YANKEE

Yankee Folk

EDWIN VALENTINE MITCHELL

The Vanguard Press, Inc.
New York

for
Polly and Bill

Foreword

For information and help in the writing of this book I am deeply indebted to a number of persons, especially to Barrows Mussey for his aid in connection with the chapters on Yankee printers and tinkers, and for many other suggestions and the loan of books. Grateful acknowledgment is also made to former Governor Wilbert Snow of Connecticut, Archie V. Leland, Stillman D. Hitchcock, and to my uncle, the late William A. Clark. I am likewise greatly obliged to Miss Elsie Cleveland and Miss Annetta Clark. Once again I am indebted to the staff of the Connecticut Historical Society in Hartford and to that of the American History Room of the New York Public Library. For all kinds of aid I owe my best thanks to Terry West Mitchell.

E. V. M.

Contents

Illustrations

Publishing Yankees

COUNTRY YANKEES, especially from the northern tier of New England states, enjoy cultivating a reputation for taciturnity. But give them a pen or a few cases of type, and they flood the nation with their outpourings. Even New England understatement tends to give way.

My friend Barrows Mussey, to whom I am indebted for many details in this chapter, has called my attention to a passage in *A Book for Massachusetts Children*, by Hosea Hildreth, published at Boston in 1829.

"Dear child, From the letters I have written concerning the Commonwealth of Massachusetts, you have learned, that the people of this State are highly favored. . . . The principal things that make Massachusetts a good land to live in, are these;—We have the Bible, which teaches the will of God, and the way of salvation by Jesus Christ; we have the Sabbath, or Lord's Day, which affords the people an opportunity for meet-

3

ing together to worship God, and to hear the Gospel preached; we have schools of various kinds, at which our sons and daughters may acquire so much good learning as to be fitted for useful employment; we have Sabbath Schools for the instruction of children and young persons in the Bible, and in all their duty to God and mankind; we have a free and good government, which the people have established by their own authority and will; and we have good laws for the preservation of order, uprightness, and peace. . . . Now if the children of Massachusetts were all good, and behaved toward God, toward their parents, toward one another, and toward all persons, as children ought to behave, then we should have the happiest Commonwealth on the face of the earth. . . . I suppose you are satisfied, that a Commonwealth made up of good people, must be happy and prosperous; but then you are old enough to know, that there are many wicked people in Massachusetts, and that there are many children who are naughty, and who are very likely to be wicked persons, when they are grown up. This is true; but it is no good reason why you should be naughty and wicked. . . . Some children are naughty from want of instruction; but you must remember that you have had instruction, and if you behave ill, it will not be for want of knowing your duty. Ill conduct in you will be the more sinful on account of the good instruction you have had. (Signed) AN AFFECTIONATE FATHER."

The publishers of this were predecessors of the present firm of Little, Brown and Company, which I venture to guess has never done anything that would add to the wickedness of Massachusetts. But the first really towering figure among New England publishers, Isaiah Thomas of Worcester, cannot have satisfied Hosea Hildreth at all.

Losing his father not long after birth at Boston in 1749, Thomas had to pick up an education working in a printing shop. He was put to typesetting at the age of eight, and his master stood him on a box so that he could reach the case. The indefatigable research of the American Antiquarian Society, which Thomas founded, has unearthed a copy of the ballad that was little Isaiah's first effort as a compositor. It was called "The Lawyer's Pedigree," and makes one think of Ogden Nash's song about the Four Prominent Love-Children. I do not even dare guess what Hosea Hildreth must have said to the ballad. I will only remark that some years ago, when the *New York Times Book Review* inadvertently reproduced it as an illustration, it had to be scraped into illegibility on the rotogravure plate before the *Times* thought its *Book Review* fit to print.

Thomas did not get on well with his master, who was a shiftless loafer. The apprentice slipped away to try his luck in Nova Scotia in 1766, but resented the Stamp Act so fiercely that he found it prudent to come back to Boston. He also roamed southward. In 1770, however, the industrious apprentice Thomas actually became the idle master Zechariah Fowle's partner at Boston. That year he established the *Massachusetts Spy* newspaper, and so rendered himself utterly odious to the British.

Five years later the British regulars occupied Boston. On the night of April 16 Thomas sneaked his printing outfit away from Boston and took it to Worcester, which was to be his home for the rest of his life. He hurried back to join Paul Revere and others in rousing "every Middlesex village and farm." He fought as a Minuteman at Lexington and Concord.

The publishing business was too much to struggle with

for the next three years, but in 1778 he resumed the *Spy* at Worcester. Country printers generally depended for a living on their newspapers and on job printing. Thomas, however, put most of his energy into book publishing. At the height of his activity, about 1800, he had in Worcester a hundred and fifty workmen, seven presses, a paper mill, a bindery, and a share in a drugstore, where I would half like to think he sold his overstock.

Books are unhandy things to transport through snow-banks and mud wallows, as everyone learns by experimenting with even a school bag full. Thomas had a better idea. He sent his apprentices out to the four points of the compass, and set them up in business as his partners. He controlled book and newspaper publishing firms in Boston, Newburyport, and Brookfield, Massachusetts; Portsmouth and Walpole, New Hampshire; Windsor, Vermont; Albany, and Baltimore. For over a generation scarcely a New England printer or editor but had learned his trade from Thomas or an ex-apprentice of Thomas's.

To one like myself who has been a publisher, the most remarkable thing about Thomas is that he died rich and respected. He was a rather astringent old dandy, and divorced two of his three wives. Retiring with a fortune in 1802, Thomas set to work on his *History of Printing in America*. His son, Isaiah, Jr., published it for him in 1810. The past hundred and thirty-eight years have seen some additions and a few corrections; but if you want the best history of American printing, you will still have to hunt for a copy of Thomas.

Thomas was a truly public-spirited scholar. Once he had finished with the materials for his history, he intended to preserve them for other people's use. In 1812 he established and endowed the American Antiquarian

Society at Worcester, giving it not only money and a building but his now priceless collections. The Society is one of the oldest, strongest, and withal liveliest forces in American scholarship. Hardly any historian can write a chapter without owing acknowledgments to it.

When I say lively, I mean just that. Naturally the Society wants a copy of every item its founder printed or published, and it has very nearly turned the trick. It is now in the home stretch on the crowning rarity of them all, a book of which old Isaiah kept no copy. He did use some discarded sheets of it, marbled over, to bind ledgers and diaries. With learned patience the employees of the Society have gathered sheet after sheet, bleached off the marbling, and if they have not got the whole book now, it is only a question of time before they will assemble a complete Isaiah Thomas edition of *Fanny Hill, or The Memoirs of a Woman of Pleasure*. When they do that, Hosea Hildreth will revolve in his grave.

Another prolific old New England publisher was John Prentiss of Keene, New Hampshire. Prentiss blew into Keene at the age of twenty-one in 1799. He bought a local printing outfit for five dollars down and the small balance in installments, paying a lawyer fifteen cents to draw up the papers. Five dollars was a pretty fair down payment, since the *Sentinel* had a subscription list of only seventy at $1.50 a year, which was usually paid—if at all—in wood, cheese, or grain. Prentiss also carried books and stationery, and ran a circulating library. His first important enterprise as a book publisher was an edition of Isaac Watts hymns. On this he made a profit of forty dollars, with which he bought a grandfather clock for his new household.

Prentiss was a natural-born pillar of society, a Unitar-

ian, member of the school board, prohibitionist, town
official, state legislator, and a leading Freemason for
seventy-seven years. Naturally enough he would soon start
publishing school books. Salma Hale, his fellow pillar of
Keene and colleague on the school board, wrote a history
of the United States that Prentiss published and sold
endless thousands of. Prentiss's best item, the *Arithmetic*
of Daniel Adams, is a veritable nuisance to the New
England bookhunter, who often has to scramble into
attics over knee-high mounds of dilapidated *Adamses*. In
a good year Prentiss would sell as many as a hundred
thousand of these *Arithmetics*.

Printing so many books was an achievement, and bind-
ing them was practically impossible, but somehow Prentiss
contrived to get it done, setting up one large binder in
business and keeping others on a dead run. The firm he
launched as a bindery still conducts a bookstore in Keene.

When Prentiss was seventy-two, he attended the Convention of 1850 at Frankfort on the Main that tried to
settle the troubles of a disrupted Germany. He wrote
home reports of the proceedings to the *Sentinel,* in which
they were printed and, I suppose, read as a sort of public
duty to a grand old man. But if the people back home
meant thus to brighten John Prentiss's declining years,
they were being a mite hasty. The Reverend Dr. Barstow
conducted memorial services after the assassination of
Lincoln in 1865, and John Prentiss was one of five people
there that day who had attended the memorial services
for Washington in the same church in December of 1799.
Prentiss did not really begin to decline much until 1873,
when he gave up in disgust and died at ninety-five.

It is a commonplace to say that either the New England
climate was salubrious or else it killed off the unfit at an

early age. New Hampshire had another publisher whose business was less fortunate than Prentiss's, but who lived to be as old, and in his way perhaps led a fuller life. Simeon Ide, born in Shrewsbury, Massachusetts, in 1794, spent most of his youth in various parts of Vermont. He was away from his mother for two years, and when at the age of eight he rejoined her, he pulled some silver pieces out of his pocket: "There, Marm, I've saved so much."

Ide started to learn the printer's trade as soon as he was fifteen. In 1812, after his father refused to let him enlist, he took a job in the printing office of a Federalist newspaper, the Windsor, Vermont, *Washingtonian*. The Ides were fierce Republicans, so Simeon would work only on books; he would not set a word of the odious newspaper. Even this did not satisfy his father, who wrote, "I am sorry to learn you are in that dirty business and place. . . . The Mosaic rules, I fear, will not cleanse the man that touches the loathsome Press, the *Washingtonian*."

Simeon, ordered to come home at once, retorted that he was only setting up type for the Constitution and Washington's Farewell Address, "than which nothing can be better calculated to form correct principles." He stayed

on, then worked for various other Vermont masters.
While he was working for William Fessenden of Brattleboro, he used to put in overtime stitching almanacs. With
the proceeds he bought his mother a quarto Bible, which
she read through for the last time at eighty-nine, without
glasses.

Those were Biblical times. Ide's own first independent
venture was Bible publishing. His wandering father had
come to rest at New Ipswich, New Hampshire, and Simeon refitted the farm blacksmith shop for a printing office.
All he needed then was type, a press, and paper. The third
of April, 1815, he went on horseback to Boston, feeling
very much the country jay. But he bought for a hundred
and twenty dollars the press on which Munroe and Francis
had printed the first illustrated set of Shakespeare's plays
issued in America, and he bought three hundred and fifty
pounds of bourgeois type (modern nine-point).

In this type his eleven-year-old sister set up the New
Testament, while Simeon worked the old hand press. A
paper mill in Peterboro charged him outrageous prices
for paper, and he had to sell a thousand copies of the
finished product below cost at twenty-eight cents a copy
to the New Hampshire Bible Society to meet the bill. He
swapped off some more in Boston for sixty dollars' worth
of hardware and leather, which he sold to a cousin in
the saddlery business.

He wound up his sales trip by working a while in Boston, then looked around for a place to start a newspaper.
Keene seemed promising until he discovered John Prentiss. Brattleboro had his old bosses, the firm of Holbrook
and Fessenden, who were equally entrenched, but gen-
erously refrained from discouraging him. Ide launched the
Yeoman in February, 1817, and built his subscription list

up to four hundred within a year, after which he had a
chance to buy out one of his old masters at Windsor,
Vermont, and moved north.

So far as business went, Windsor was the high point of
Ide's life. In sixteen years of running a newspaper, printing shop, bindery, and book publishing business, he printed
nearly eighty books and pamphlets, and accumulated a
comfortable fortune.

One stray item from his Windsor newspaper: A man
named Simeon Cary was fined for selling rum by the
gill. He thereupon got a tin tube three feet long, holding
a pint, and sold rum with impunity by the yard. Possibly
this perfidy was among the reasons that induced Ide to
become, like John Prentiss, an ardent temperance man.

By 1834, Ide was so prosperous as to be good picking
for some promoters at Claremont, New Hampshire, who
persuaded him to become the "agent" or general manager
of the new Claremont Manufacturing Company. The company took over Ide's printing and publishing business, ran
a rather unsuccessful paper mill, and for a while also
made textiles. But the panic of 1837 and the unscrupulous
stupidity of the company directors prevented Ide from
accomplishing anything permanent.

In 1841, for instance, he contracted with Noah Webster for the exclusive publication of Webster's *Spellers*
and *Unabridged Dictionary*. Forgetting the dictionary,
the speller is estimated to have sold thirty million copies
between 1783 and 1860, and another thirty-odd million
up to 1890. Whereupon the creditors of the company
called in a ten-thousand-dollar loan, attached the stock-
holders' property, and killed the Webster contract.

In 1858, when Ide was sixty-four, he got tired of his
business connections at Claremont and resigned from the

company. He started to print books again for a Boston publisher, but the Civil War spoiled that. He tried a job running a paper mill in Auburn, New York, for a week, collected twenty-five dollars for his work and expenses, and sent it all back to Claremont to pay a laborer to whom he was indebted. After a very unfortunate experience with an Auburn newspaper publisher, he had to borrow the fare to New York from his daughters; and in New York, aged sixty-nine, he went back to typesetting at ten dollars a week.

Then kind friends in New York lent him stereotyping equipment, and in two years he saved up six hundred dollars. His numerous children in Claremont, meanwhile, kept wanting him to come home and live with them; but the only way they could fetch him was to put him in the way of buying the *Claremont National Eagle*. For its plant and four hundred subscribers he paid sixteen hundred dollars. He ran the paper for four years, doubled the subscription list, hired girls to set type while he himself pulled the hand press as he had done at New Ipswich fifty-one years before, and sold out at a profit of thirty-six hundred dollars. He went on with book and job printing for a few years more.

When he was eighty-five he threw away his glasses, as his mother had done, and read with the naked eye. This was two years after his celebrated prank of walking from Claremont to Chester, Vermont, some twenty-seven miles, and then giving the Fourth of July oration at Chester. At eighty-six he wrote a valuable little book, now very rare, about the exploits of his brother George Brown Ide and his Bear Flag Party in California. His ninetieth birthday he celebrated by walking across the newly opened Brooklyn Bridge. And his ninety-fifth was his last.

It would take a five-foot shelf of such volumes as this to sketch the lives of Yankee printers who went west and grew up with the country. Just one of them I cannot refrain from including, because, after all, he did not go so very far west—only to Albany—and, besides, he put one of New England's favorite occupations on an industrial basis. This printer was Joel Munsell. He was born at Northfield, Massachusetts, in 1808, and learned the printing trade across the Connecticut at Greenfield. He was nineteen when the western fever caught him, and he spent the rest of his life in Albany as a successful commercial printer. But he took an interest in the art and history of his own trade almost unknown in those days, and exceedingly rare in these. His chronology of paper-making became a standard work like Thomas's *Printing in America,* and, in fact, Munsell published a second edition of Thomas.

None of these worthy achievements would be enough to drag Munsell back across the Hudson boundary line. I tell of him because he carried with him to the west the New England passion so clearly recalled by Edward Everett Hale: "At the elders' table great talk about genealogy: whether Gib Atkins did or did not leave a particular bit of land to certain successors who now own it; whether the Picos and the Robbs were on good terms after the marriage of one of them to an Everett. I will say, in passing, that, as we grew older, we children had the wit to introduce these subjects for the purpose of seeing the mad rage with which different aged cousins advanced to the attack, as a bull might to a red flag."

Munsell was the leading genealogical publisher of his time, and for three years he actually issued—in Albany!— the sacrosanct *New England Historical and Genealogical*

Register. He thus made the ancestry of the few available to the prying scholarship of the many.

The greatest publishers Boston, and in their way perhaps the country, has ever seen, were not proper Bostonians. William Davis Ticknor and his partner James T. Fields both came down from New Hampshire, Ticknor from up next to Dartmouth, Fields from the metropolis of Portsmouth. Oddly enough, the Connecticut Valley rustic spent some years as a broker and banker in State Street before his sense of literary vocation ran away with his financial judgment, whereas Fields arrived from Portsmouth at the age of fourteen to work in a bookstore because of his quaint notion that booksellers read books all day.

Ticknor, fresh from his desk at the Columbian Bank, bought out the publishing house of Carter, Hendee and Company in 1832. Carter and Hendee's was the shop where Fields had just begun learning that most booksellers have to spend a lot of time over account books. Afterward he lived in Ticknor's household along with another prominent Boston publisher-to-be, Thomas Niles, who induced Louisa May Alcott to write *Little Women*.

In 1845 Ticknor took Fields into partnership. In 1859 the *Atlantic Monthly* came on the market, and Ticknor very reluctantly put in a ten-thousand-dollar bid for it just five minutes before the legal deadline. Fields was abroad, and showed only resignation when he heard of the purchase. Within two years he found himself replacing James Russell Lowell as editor, and held the job until William Dean Howells took it over in 1871.

The famous New England authors whom Ticknor and Fields published were so many that the very list is wearisome—Holmes, Thoreau, Emerson, Whittier, and Long-

fellow were the biggest. Hawthorne could scarcely buy
a railroad ticket without Ticknor to shepherd him. The
firm accomplished something that probably no other
American publisher has ever done: It convinced the liter-
ate public that any book bound in dirty-brown embossed
cloth with *T &F* on the backbone was certain to be good
of its kind. A remark to this effect by one of his professors
first interested another great American publisher—I think
it was Henry Holt—in the book business.

Ticknor died in 1864, Fields in 1881. Their business,
after several changes of style, fell into the hands of a
printer boy from barren northern Vermont, who had first
squeaked out a living in Boston as a free-lance proofreader
and copy editor in 1846.

Only two years after this thin beginning, Henry Oscar
Houghton was a boss printer, working largely for Little,
Brown and Company and Ticknor and Fields. Book publishers have a tradition that to combine printing and publishing is sure ruin for both branches; but Houghton started
a printing firm in 1864, the year Ticknor died, and Houghton printer and Houghton publisher have been linked ever
since. H. O. Houghton & Company, however, remains a
separate corporation and carries as much weight as does
the publishing house of Houghton Mifflin.

No doubt Simeon Ide was too busy building up the
Claremont National Eagle to worry about might-have-
beens; still, I never see a Merriam-Webster dictionary
printed at the Riverside Press without thinking that avari-
cious creditors usually overreach themselves. The Riverside Press got the job in 1864. It has been printing
Webster dictionaries for eighty-four years now, and will
probably continue for as long again. Yankees have always preferred to shop where their grandfathers did.

Star Watchers

ROBERT FROST wrote a poem about a New Hampshire man he knew who, failing as a farmer, burned down his farmhouse for the fire insurance and with the proceeds bought a telescope for six hundred dollars, to satisfy a lifelong curiosity about the stars.

New England has always had its stargazers. There is hardly a place of any size that hasn't a telescope of respectable dimensions, the property of some local academy or other institution, or of some individual interested in astronomy. One private observatory I know is on a small island off the coast of Maine, where the planets and brighter stars make pathways of light on the water, and the watcher has an unobstructed view of vast sweeps of sky.

For many years a little man in a derby and a short tan box coat used to stand beside a fair-sized telescope which on clear nights he set up on Main Street opposite the old State House in Hartford, Connecticut. His name was

John Hale, and the telescope he used was a seven-inch brass-tube affair. He usually hung a card on the instrument with the name of the planet—Venus, Mars, Jupiter —on which his telescope was trained, and he said to passers-by, "A view of the celestial heavens, ten cents."

Dr. Oliver Wendell Holmes said that after he had a ten-cent look at the transit of Venus through a telescope on the Mall in Boston, the earth was to him wholly different from what it had been. "I knew from books what a speck it is in the universe, but nothing brought the fact home to me like the sight of the sister planet sailing across the sun's disk, about large enough for a buckshot, not large enough for a full-sized bullet."

Most of the old New England street astronomers are now with the farthest of the far stars, but New England still holds a leading place in the telescope trade. The famous firm of Alvan Clark and Sons has been making telescopes for more than a century. For many years they produced the world's largest and best lenses. Astronomical telescopes come in two styles—refractors, which focus the rays of incoming light through a lens, and reflectors, which employ a concave mirror to collect the light. The Clarks made refractors, but there is a size beyond which this type of telescope cannot be made. One of the technical reasons for this is that the lens has to be held in position at the rim and the weight of a large refractor may be too great to be supported in this way. The glass has a tendency to buckle under its own weight. But with a mirror this difficulty is not encountered because it can be securely supported from beneath. The 200-inch mirror of the giant telescope on Mount Palomar, California, which is twice the size of the huge Mount Wilson reflector, weighs fourteen and a half tons and is mounted in a 375-ton cradle.

Obviously a lens of this size could not be supported at its thin edge at the top end of a telescope. The Clarks probably reached the limit for a refractor when they made the 40-inch glass for the Yerkes Observatory.

Alvan Clark, the founder of the firm, was born in Ashfield, Massachusetts, in 1804. He was a direct descendant of Thomas Clark, the mate of the "Mayflower," who as a mariner must have had some interest in the stars. At seventeen Clark went to work as a wagon maker, but, as he had a talent for drawing, he soon began offering his services in the neighboring hill towns of western Massachusetts in the execution of small portraits, some in pen and ink and some in water colors. He said he met with a pretty satisfactory measure of success.

In 1824 a small incident changed his plans. Wanting some fine sable-hair brushes for miniature work, he sent to Boston for them by a man who was in the habit of visiting the city. The brushes came wrapped in a piece of newspaper bearing an advertisement that caught young Clark's eye. It was headed, "Engravers Wanted." He was not long in making up his mind to apply for the job. On reaching Boston with samples of his work, he found that engravers were wanted for calico printing at the Merrimac Works in East Chelmsford, near Lowell. He was hired at $8.00 a week for the first year, and $9.00 a week for the next three years.

He was married in 1826, supplementing his wages in the engraving shop by painting and cutting stamps. Soon after, his employers transferred him to Providence, then to New York, where he remained until 1832, when he moved back to New England, this time to Fall River, Massachusetts. All this time he was engaged as a textile engraver. In New York he had an opportunity to study

art and practiced all he could. His next move was to Cambridgeport, across the Charles River from Boston. Here in 1836 he bought a house and for a number of years supported his family by painting portraits and miniatures in Boston. His work was favorably known for likeness and finish.

Clark first became interested in telescopes through his son, George Bassett Clark, who was born in Lowell in 1827. In 1844, George, who had been studying civil engineering for some time at Andover Academy, happened to read an account of casting and grinding reflectors for telescopes and, before he even mentioned the matter to his father, had procured some metal and made a small casting for a mirror. The elder Clark was immediately interested and began an intensive study of what had been done in this curious art, so that his son could have the benefit of his maturer judgment in giving effect to his experiments.

"About this time," Alvan Clark wrote, "the great telescope at Harvard College Observatory was put to use, and greatly did I wish to see it and look through it, but Prof. Bond informed me that I must come with an order from President Everett before this could be allowed. This order was speedily obtained. I was far enough advanced in knowledge of such matters to perceive and locate the errors of figure in their fifteen-inch glass at first sight, yet these were very small, just enough to leave me in full possession of all the hope and courage needed to give me a start, especially when informed that this object glass alone cost $12,000."

"I began," he further said, "by reworking some old and poor object glasses of small instruments, there being no material in our market of suitable quality, and, after gaining confidence . . . sufficient, as I thought, to warrant the outlay, I imported one pair of disks of five and one-quarter inches, and found others in New York of larger size, even up to eight inches, of very good quality."

This Yankee portrait painter was forty when he founded the house of Alvan Clark and Sons, telescope makers. They made a few instruments to order and sold some which they made on their own account; but the encouragement was small at first, until Alvan Clark began to report his astronomical findings to Reverend W. R. Dawes, the famous double-star observer in England. Clark gave him the position of two new double stars he had discovered with a glass four and three-quarter inches in diameter. One of the stars was Sextantis.

In 1853 the Clarks finished a glass of seven and one half inches aperture, with which the elder Clark made further discoveries in the heavens, which he reported to Mr. Dawes, who bought the glass and later four others. Reports concerning the performance of these lenses published by Mr. Dawes in the monthly notices of the Royal Astronomical Society were of great help to the Clarks in procuring orders. In the delicate and arduous work of grinding and polishing lenses these New Englanders showed extraordinary skill, their instruments meeting the most exacting standards of optical accuracy. When the excellence of the Clark instruments became known, the sales of their telescopes to Europe and America increased.

In 1859 Alvan Clark visited Mr. Dawes in England, who took him to Greenwich Observatory, and to a meeting of the Royal Astronomical Society, at which he met Sir John Herschel and other distinguished astronomers.

Meanwhile, Alvan Clark's younger son, Alvan G. Clark, who was born in Fall River, July 10, 1832, and under whom the firm was to achieve its greatest fame, entered the business with his father and brother. He was twenty years old. Educated in the public schools of Cambridge, Massachusetts, whence the family had moved when he was very young, he, too, as a boy, showed an aptitude for everything requiring keen vision and exactness. He was deeply interested in astronomy while still in school, and won prizes for treatises on the casting and grinding of specula.

In 1860 the firm received its first order for a big lens to be used in the United States. Dr. F. A. P. Barnard, who later became president of Columbia but was then chief of the University of Mississippi, ordered a telescope that was to be larger than any refractor ever used. The rough glass for this eighteen-and-one-half-inch telescope came from Birmingham, England, early in 1862. Within a year young Alvan G. Clark, while testing the lens, discovered the companion to Sirius. For this discovery and for his work in making astronomical instruments, particularly large telescopes, he was awarded a medal by the French Academy of Sciences. The Clarks, who had built a factory in Cambridge in the summer of 1860 to accommodate their expanding business, were prevented by the Civil War from delivering the Mississippi telescope, and it was sold to the Astronomical Society of Chicago.

Prior to this, the largest size telescopes made by the Clarks were two twelve-inch objectives, one for the Austrian Observatory at Vienna, the other for Wesleyan University at Middletown, Connecticut. Inquiry concerning this last telescope brought word that it was replaced about 1922, and the old Clark instrument sold to Miami University at Oxford, Ohio. An eleven-inch instrument was also made by the Clarks for the Observatory at Lisbon, Portugal.

As soon as the Clarks had shown that effective telescopes with apertures two feet or more in diameter could be made, Congress was asked to authorize the purchase of a lens for the National Observatory at Washington, which was equipped with nothing more formidable than an old Munich refractor of nine and one half inches. A bill was passed in 1870 empowering the director of the observatory to contract for the largest size telescope of American manufacture. It was decided that the glass should measure twenty-six inches, and the contract for it was awarded to Alvan Clark and Sons. Difficulty was experienced in obtaining the proper glass of the right size for the job. The rough disks did not reach Boston from Paris until December, 1871, but the grinding and polishing were finished the following October. In November, 1873, the complete telescope was ready for use. For this instrument the Clarks were paid $46,000 in gold, which was far in excess of the paper currency of the period.

Another order for a twenty-six-inch glass was received at the same time from L. J. McCormick of Chicago. Among other lenses made by the firm were the twelve-inch for Victoria University, twelve and one half inches for Morrison, fifteen and one half inches for Wisconsin, sixteen inches for Warren Observatory, eighteen and one half inches for Northwestern University, twenty inches for Denver, twenty-three inches for Princeton, twenty-six inches for Virginia, thirty inches for St. Petersburg Imperial Observatory, and thirty-six inches for Lick Observatory. This last lens was at the time the largest and most powerful glass in the world. Alvan G. Clark died in 1887, after it was completed but before it was installed.

The next great telescope made by the Clarks was one purchased by Charles T. Yerkes of Chicago for the University of Chicago. This instrument was originally intended for the University of Southern California. When the great Lick Observatory telescope was installed, the people of Southern California, not wishing to be outdone, resolved that they would place a bigger one atop Wilson's peak near Los Angeles. There was a boom on in that section of California at the time, and the money was readily subscribed, but while the Clarks were making the telescope the boom suffered a setback, and people failed to pay their subscriptions. It was then that Professor Hale of Kenwood Observatory recommended the purchase of the lens to Mr. Yerkes, a patron of the university, and he bought it for $100,000. The objective glass for this telescope measured forty inches in diameter, with a maximum thickness of three and one half feet. It is still the largest refractor in the world.

Alvan G. Clark was the only surviving member of the original firm when the Yerkes lens was made. He worried greatly over the undertaking. The transportation of the lens to the observatory gave him many anxious hours. The glass was wrapped in flannel and cotton batting and packed in a box padded with curled hair. The box, fixed on springs, was placed in a parlor car for the journey. After he had delivered it, Mr. Clark said he felt as if he had been relieved of a crushing load. He spoke of retiring from business. The fatigue of the journey proved too much for him. In a little more than a week after his return he died unexpectedly at his home in Cambridge on June 10, 1897.

A woman contemporary of the Clarks in nineteenth-century New England who had a good deal to do with

telescopes was Maria Mitchell, the Nantucket astronomer. The daughter of Quaker parents, she was born
August 1, 1818, on Nantucket Island, where she lived
more than half her life and achieved international fame
as an astronomer. Her inheritance and the insular environment in which she was reared combined to give her
a taste and disposition for scientific studies, especially
those relating to navigation.

For during the early part of the last century the Nantucket whalers rounded Cape Horn and stood out across
the vast watery wastes of the Pacific Ocean, where a high
degree of skill and knowledge in taking observations from
the stars was necessary to trace the ships' courses. It was
then the ruling passion of every Nantucket boy to study
navigation. At the Friends Monthly Meeting school little
children, instead of learning the catechism, were taught
to box the compass.

Maria's father, William Mitchell, was an amateur astronomer, schoolmaster, and bank cashier. Captains of
whaling ships before leaving port brought their chronometers to the Mitchell house in Vestal Street to be rated
and set to Greenwich time. So expertly did William Mitchell do this that he finally became the rater of all the
chronometers of the entire Nantucket whaling fleet of
ninety-two vessels. This made it necessary for him to take
observations on every fine day of the year. Astronomical
talk was common in the Mitchell home while Maria was
growing up.

During the annular eclipse of 1831, William Mitchell
enlisted Maria's aid when he made his observations. A
child of twelve and a half at the time, and a student in her
father's school, she sat beside the chronometer and noted
the seconds of beginning and end. The practical object

of these observations, which were made concurrently with others taken at Dorchester and Monomoy, was to determine the longitude of the Vestal Street house where the whaling ships' chronometers were set.

On the approach of Halley's Comet in 1835, there was great rivalry among astronomers to be the first to spot the celestial visitor. It was still a very faint telescopic object when rediscovered at Yale College and then Nantucket. Maria Mitchell maintained until her dying day that her father was the very first to find it. In any case, being among the foremost to see the comet gave the Vestal Street lookout the status of an observatory, and drew the attention of prominent astronomers to the stargazing Mitchell family.

Maria showed such a marked aptitude for mathematics that while she was still in her teens an attempt was made to get her to open a navigation school at Nantucket. Bowditch's *Navigator* was the Bible of all young Nantucketers fitting to go to sea, but these youths, of course, knew nothing of the higher mathematics behind the practical navigation formulas in the book. Maria, however, was not satisfied with merely knowing how to work the tables; she wanted to know how they were constructed. Professor Benjamin Peirce had not then published his *Explanation of the Navigator and Almanac,* and, before Maria was able to construct the astronomical tables herself, she was obliged to study many scientific works, including the reports of mathematical societies. Despite her qualifications to teach navigation, she declined to open a school.

In 1837, when she was nineteen, Maria was made librarian of the Nantucket Athenaeum, of which her father was president for more than thirty years. This institution,

which was incorporated in 1834, contained a library of
several thousand volumes and a museum stuffed with miscellaneous curiosities consisting chiefly of barbaric weapons, dresses, and utensils brought by the whale ships
from the South Seas. The library was open only a limited
number of hours each week, which gave Maria an opportunity for uninterrupted study and reading. Here she
read Laplace and studied Bowditch's Appendix to the
third volume of the *Mécanique Céleste*, which treats of
the orbits of comets, and read Gauss's *Theoria Motus* in
the original Latin text. In the disastrous fire of 1846,
which wiped out the business section of Nantucket, the
Greek temple that housed the library and all the books
inside were destroyed. But people in other parts of New
England, moved by Nantucket's plight, contributed toward rebuilding the Athenaeum, and under Maria's direction the library was soon better than it had been before
the disaster.

During the seventeen years of her librarianship, Maria
advanced in knowledge and was of great assistance to her
father, whose scientific reputation was steadily increas-
ing. He was made an Overseer of Harvard College, serving on the Observatory Committee, part of the time as
chairman. In 1836 he became cashier of the Pacific Bank
at Nantucket, and the family moved from the Vestal
Street house to the bank building on Main Street. William
Mitchell or his daughter or both together were often seen
on the roof of the bank as they made their observations.
When her father was obliged to go away on business or
other trips, Maria continued the sequence of his observations. Mr. Mitchell bought an efficient telescope and a
large celestial globe. In addition, they had the use of
numerous instruments loaned by the state and the federal

government on condition that they furnish certain data for various official surveys. Massachusetts supplied a transit for the meridian, West Point Academy sent a repeating circle, and the Coast Survey an equatorial telescope and transit instrument for the prime vertical, "the understanding being that the observatory at Nantucket should be one end of a great arc in the determination of the figure of the earth." In this way the small island observatory came to be rather well equipped.

In a biographical notice of Maria written by her brother, Henry Mitchell, who had a distinguished career as a hydrographer, the work of the two astronomers at this period is thus described:

"For several years father and daughter worked together on routine observations of the cumulative sort, much relied upon in those days as cancelling errors which modern improvements in instruments and methods have more effectually corrected. They observed moon culminations and occultations for longitude, and the transit of stars across the prime vertical for latitude, until, towards the last, they obtained a zenith telescope. The aspects of the planets, the solar spots, meteors, and auroral clouds, were observed diligently. But in 1845, when Smyth's *Celestial Cycle* (containing the Bedford Catalogue) appeared, they entered upon systematic studies of nebulae and double stars, using often two telescopes side by side on the top of the Pacific Bank. Thenceforth they were prospectors beyond the frontiers; and routine work gave place to exciting explorations."

Stars and domes have long been a standard feature of poetry, and it is not surprising to find that the thoughts of astronomers have sometimes trended toward romantic verse. Maria's frequently strayed in that direction while she waited on the rooftop for the transit of stars. She was fond of repeating verses, even composing them herself, and it is probable that she viewed with leniency the poetic efforts of Admiral Smyth, author of the *Celestial Cycle*. When eventually she met this ancient mariner in England, he asked her if his book had reached as far as her island home.

"If it is a fine night at Nantucket," she said, "my father has your catalogue open upon his table, and runs in every few minutes from his telescope to identify his objects."

Gratified at hearing this, he then told her that his forte was poetry, and presented her with some verses which he had printed himself on a small press, because "the publisher could not appreciate their merits."

The long night watches which Maria kept on the roof of the Pacific Bank, patiently scanning the heavens with her telescope, were at length rewarded. The discovery of three comets in advance of their announcements, but not quite in time for her to be proclaimed their discoverer, raised her hopes. And then one night in the fall of 1847, a strange new object came within the field of her glass. She immediately determined its position and the following night observed it again, when the object was found to be in motion among the stars. Maria Mitchell had discovered a brand new comet.

It was thought at first that the comet had been seen in other parts of the world before Maria sighted it at Nantucket, but after considerable correspondence her claim to being the discoverer was established, and King Frederic VI of Denmark awarded her the gold medal he had founded to be given "to any person who should first discover a telescopic comet." Many distinguished persons championed her in this claim, the correspondence in her behalf being chiefly conducted by Edward Everett, who wrote an interesting introductory note to the published letters which reads in part as follows:

"On the first of October, 1847, at half past ten o'clock P.M., a telescopic comet was discovered by Miss Maria Mitchell of Nantucket, nearly vertical above Polaris about five degrees. . . . On the 3rd of October the same comet was seen at half past seven, P.M., at Rome, by Father de Vico, and information of the fact was immediately communicated by him to Professor Schumacher at Altona. On the 7th day of October, at twenty minutes past nine, P.M., it was observed by Mr. W. R. Dawes, at Camden Lodge, Cranbrook, Kent, in England, and on the 11th it was seen by Madame Rümker, the wife of the Director of the Observatory at Hamburg. Mr. Schumacher in announcing this last discovery observes, 'Madam Rümker has for several years been on the lookout for comets, and her persevering industry seemed at last about to be rewarded, when a letter was received from Father de Vico, addressed to the editor of this journal, from which it appeared that the same comet had been observed by him on the 3rd instant at Rome.'

"Not deeming it probable that his daughter had anticipated the observers of this country and Europe in the discovery of this comet, no steps were taken by Mr. Mitchell with a view to obtaining the King of Denmark's medal. Prompt information, however, of the discovery was transmitted by Mr. Mitchell to his friend, William C. Bond, Esq., Director of the Observatory at Cambridge. The observations of the Messrs. Bond upon the comet commenced on the 7th of October; and on the 30th were transmitted by me to Mr. Schumacher, for publica-

tion in the *Astronomische Nachrichten*. It was stated in
the memorandum of the Messrs. Bond, that the comet
was seen by Miss Mitchell on the 1st instant. This notice
appeared in the *Nachrichten* of December 9, 1847, and
the priority of Miss Mitchell's discovery was immediately
admitted throughout Europe."

Maria was still in her twenties when she discovered the
comet which was named for her. Henry Mitchell, writing
of her at this time, said, "It was found that she was not
only fully able to make all the observations and computa-
tions required for locating celestial objects, but she could
compute their orbits and predict their reappearance in our
skies. The European astronomers came to feel a personal
interest in her; and when, some years later, she crossed the
ocean, she became the honored guest of the most learned
men in Europe, and visited all the observatories as a
privileged inspector of their instruments and their methods."

It was on her return to Nantucket from her first European tour that Miss Elizabeth Peabody, "representing
the women of America," presented her with a fine telescope made by Alvan Clark. Maria Mitchell, incidentally,
took an active and prominent part in the woman's movement of her time.

Following her discovery of the comet many honors
were bestowed upon her. In 1849 she accepted an appointment as one of the computers of the Nautical Almanac, an office which she held for nearly twenty years,
her work in this connection being confined mainly to the
astronomical part of the almanac. Her special assign-
ment was the planet Venus.

Following the death of her mother in 1861, she and
her father left Nantucket to make their home in Lynn,

where her sister lived. Here she remained until 1865, when she was appointed Professor of Astronomy and Director of the Observatory at Vassar College. The rest of her life was spent in teaching and study at Vassar. Early in 1888 she retired and returned to Lynn, where on June twenty-eighth of the same year she died.

At one time, according to her brother, his sister's faith in a future life underwent the transient shadow of an eclipse. She asked John Greenleaf Whittier, who was also a Quaker, if he was perfectly confident of his immortality. The poet's answer was, "I cannot conceive that the soul of Maria Mitchell can ever die."

The house in Vestal Street to which the captains of the whaling ships brought their chronometers to be rated, and where at the age of twelve Maria Mitchell began her astronomical apprenticeship, is still standing. The house, with the small observatory behind it, as well as the science library across the street, are maintained by the Maria Mitchell Foundation, and anyone can visit them. Nantucket is a little place, but it is not a small thing that one of America's most distinguished women was born there.

Nantucket was also the home for a number of years of a boy genius who in all probability would have made his mark as an astronomer if he had not died at the age of twenty-two. This was Ebenezer Porter Mason, who was born December 7, 1819, in Washington, Connecticut, where his father, Reverend Stephen Mason, was pastor of the Congregational church. The boy's mother died when he was three, and the family later becoming unsettled, Ebenezer went to live with his aunt in the South. But in 1829 Mr. Mason took the pastorate of a Congregational church at Nantucket, where, finding himself pleasantly settled, he once more assembled his family

around him, including Ebenezer. The boy's first letter
from Nantucket was dated July 11, 1830, and was addressed to his aunt. It is a concise, well-written letter
coming from a boy only ten years old.

"My dear aunt—

"I have so many things to tell you, that I hardly know
where to begin. I had a very pleasant passage, and I can
say that I was not sick at all on the voyage. I intended to
go from New York on Friday evening, when I could have
company; but that very day, at dinner, I heard that there
was a sloop going to Nantucket next morning, the very
one which father and our family went in. I resolved to
go in it, but it was now four o'clock in the afternoon and
it was to sail at five. I had to pack up very quick and go
on board. I arrived here Sunday afternoon after a passage
of about two days. All Sunday there was a brisk wind
against us. When I came to the wharf, I was surprised to
see so large a city. It is nearly as large as Richmond, and
the population is between seven and eight thousand. The
place is called Nantucket. The houses are nearly all of
wood, and are painted any way, white one side, red another, green another, or some such way, and they are
for the most part covered all over with shingles. They
have walks on the top to get a view of the sea.

"There are some trees on the island. In the town they
are about as thick as on Shocco Hill in Richmond; but in
the country there are not any except a small grove for
the cattle to find shelter from the storms. The soil is
sandy, but when I rode out of town the grass was so green,
and all was so pleasant, that I never thought of the want
of trees and fences. There are a great many more ships
and vessels here than in Richmond, most of which are
engaged in the whale fishery. When I came into port they

were so thick that our sloop could hardly enter. There have been several launches here since I arrived, one of which I went to see; but as they could not prepare it till several hours afterwards, I returned. There is but one steamboat here at present, called the Marco Bozzaris, which runs twice a week between here and New Bedford.

"D. and I entered Coffin-school Monday June 28th. It is a large school, and a great many boys are idle and vicious. Nine of them were whipped yesterday afternoon. I now study Caesar, Arithmetic, Reading, and Writing.

"Our house is large, and there are rooms in the basement story, in one of which D. and I have chisels and other tools, with which we make ships, hen-coops, &c. L. has a baby-house up stairs in her room in which are about six babies, which she instructs. D. and I are both well. We have a hired servant named Martha. Her parents reside in a part of the town called New Guinea, where the blacks live, and they are a very merry set of people; and now when I wish myself in Guinea I can easily get there."

From a letter written soon after this to his uncle, Reverend J. H. Turner, one gets a further interesting glimpse of Nantucket and the character of the youthful prodigy.

"My dear uncle—

"I received your letter of September 2d, and derived much amusement from it. As for Nantucket, so far from being the 'jumping off place,' it lies exactly over the centre of the earth.

"I went to Siasconset a few weeks ago, a small town on the northeastern part of Nantucket. On the beach the sea rolls very high. It is eight or nine miles from town, composed of fishermen's houses, mostly white-washed, where the fishermen stay in the fishing season. A few of the wealthy people have handsome gardens and cottages there, where they reside in the summer season. People here are very fond of puddings: they make blackberry puddings, whortleberry puddings, and puddings of nearly everything they can be made of, including corn-puddings which they manufacture out of green corn, and I like them much.

"I hope I shall not forget my obligation to you in your old age. My house (if I have one) and all its comforts must be shared with you, and my bed also.—I have not caught a whale yet, but the first one I catch shall be sent you.

"Your affectionate nephew,
"E. P. Mason."

At the age of twelve Ebenezer surprised the headmaster of his school by an unexpected indication of his mathematical powers. A scholar in a higher class went through a demonstration that was approved as correct. It was a branch of mathematics young Mason had not studied, but as he sat near by, apparently pursuing his own studies, his attention was arrested by an error in the demonstration.

"Is that right?" he asked the preceptor.

" Right?" answered the teacher. "Why not?"

Ebenezer then took up the demonstration and went through with it, proving that the correct conclusion was entirely different from that obtained by the older boy.

About this time an incident occurred that first turned his attention to the study of astronomy. A relative who came to visit his father was wearing a pair of concave glasses and, perceiving that Ebenezer was also near-sighted, put the glasses on him. The boy was surprised and delighted as he looked about and saw, with a distinctness and beauty before unknown to him, the houses, the trees, the birds, and the people walking in the streets. That night he was permitted to look through the glasses at the heavens and was filled with ecstasy and amazement. It was the first time he had ever seen a star distinctly. Sent on an errand, he stayed out until a late hour gazing at the firmament. Soon afterward he was provided with spectacles of his own.

There is no doubt that Nantucket suited the boy very well. He studied diligently, took to writing poetry and playing chess. As he said later, "The peculiar habits of the islanders, living as it were in a little world of their own, the sun rising out of the water, and the stars reflected upon its surface in the evening, made an impression on my mind that I could never forget. If ever I was anything of a poet, it was here." His feelings on finally leaving Nantucket in 1835 were expressed in the following lines.

FAREWELL TO NANTUCKET

Thou art a barren spot of earth,
A lonely island of the sea,
And though thou'rt not my place of birth,
Thou'st been a welcome home to me.
And now, when I must leave thy shore,
I cannot go without a tear,
To think I cannot see thee more,
Nor tread thy fields to memory dear.
'Tis not alone thy soil I love,
But heave a sad and sorrowing heart,
That when from thee I far remove,
From dearest friends I too must part.

I go to distant, milder lands,
But in my bosom cherish still,
The fond remembrance of my friends—
Thou sea-girt island, Fare thee well!

At twelve Ebenezer was far enough advanced in his studies to enter Yale College, but he was two years too young, fourteen being the lowest age limit for the freshman class. He spent two years at a boys' school at Ellington, Connecticut, and did not finally present himself for examination at New Haven until August, 1835. Denison Olmsted, professor of astronomy at Yale, said, "I well remember his appearance and the impression he made on me at this time. He was in his seventeenth year, but his figure, complexion, and whole air, were those of a child of fourteen, being slender in person, complexion pale, voice soft, and whole appearance very juvenile. I was immediately struck with the superiority of his mathematical powers and attainments, from the full and luminous explanations he gave of the principles of arithmetical rules, and from the ready and correct solutions he gave of problems. I was uncommonly impressed with his adroitness in extracting roots, and in explaining the reason of each step of the process. Even in extracting the cube root, he required no figuring but soon after a case was proposed, he gave the answer by a process purely mental."

From New Haven Ebenezer wrote to his aunt that autumn, saying astronomy was still a favorite study with him and he had a telescope in his room with which to make observations. This telescope, a seven-and-one-half-foot reflector with a six-and-one-half-inch aperture, belonged to his classmate, Hamilton L. Smith of New London, who had become interested in the construction and use of telescopes before he entered college. Since the place where Smith roomed was unfitted for making observations, the two boys carried the instrument down into the street, but here they were bothered by spectators, and shifted their observation post to the platform above the portico of the chapel, where they were free from interruptions. This move made it more convenient to keep the telescope in Ebenezer's room, which gave him an opportunity to use it whenever he liked, and before the end of his freshman year he had made numerous and delicate observations.

During his sophomore year young Mason joined his friend Smith and Smith's brother in making a reflecting telescope. Guided by Mudge's *Treatise on Making Speculums for Telescopes,* they obtained the raw materials and a mold and did their own casting in the stove in their room, working until all hours of the night. They were fortunate enough to get a good rough casting the first time. The next week was spent in grinding it down. They then cemented a hone to a block of wood, shaped it to fit their gauges, and with this began giving the speculum its proper figure.

"At length," said Smith, "the momentous time arrived for the polishing. With a degree of trouble and caution we often laughed at afterwards, we formed the polisher of pitch, and set it aside to cool. We were obliged to work chiefly by night, as our college duties required our unremitted efforts during the day. After a hasty supper, therefore, we commenced the labor of polishing. The polishing powder used was the red oxide of iron, and so cautious had we been, that we had sent to New York with directions to procure the finest article at any expense, and we were fortunate in obtaining it. I scarcely need say that we afterwards prepared it for ourselves, and finally laid it aside for putty, or the combined oxides of tin and lead. As the figure of the pitch polisher had altered somewhat in casting, we commenced polishing the metal in the centre first. We worked alternately from six to ten o'clock, and although the speculum was in part brilliantly polished, it was still almost one fourth of an inch from the edge. This we carefully watched, often measuring it to see how fast we were gaining upon it. Mason and my brother, while I wrought, were stationed on each side of the polisher, all ready, when it became dry and stuck, to breathe upon it and moisten it. About eleven o'clock Mason and my brother retired, and at twelve I broke off, the speculum being now nearly completed. We had already provided a sheet-iron tube, and also an excellent plane mirror. A day or two sufficed to adjust our speculum and mirror, (to give the instrument the form of a Newtonian,) and its performance on land objects encouraged us, but the first night after we were prepared was cloudy. Mason passed the night with me, the earlier part of which (after getting our lessons) was spent adjusting our eye-pieces and getting all ready for observations. Before daylight Mason and my brother were up. Jupiter was rising in the east, and the full moon shining brightly in the west. I shall never forget the joy with which my brother ran into the room and told me to get up immediately. I was soon with them in front of the house. They had the telescope mounted on a chair, and pointed at Jupiter. It showed the planet beautifully. His disk was sharply defined, and the belts were black and distinct. Indeed this first mirror I have always considered as one of the best I ever saw."

This homemade telescope belonged to Smith, but soon

afterward the three boys constructed one for Ebenezer, but neither of these instruments was in the same class with the one Smith made toward the end of his college career with the help of Mason and another student named Bradley. This was a fourteen-foot reflector with a twelve-inch aperture. The instrument was first planned and begun in the summer of 1838 by Smith. After several failures, a reasonably good cast was made, and the polishing of the speculum finished toward the end of the summer. Smith and Bradley shared the expense and the long labor of grinding, while Mason joined in the less arduous task of giving the mirror its final polish and figure. This great telescope constructed by these three Yale students was at the time the largest and finest one ever made in the United States.

As a student of astronomy, Ebenezer more than fulfilled the promise he gave when he entered college. Endowed with extraordinary powers of observation, the skillful hand of an artist, and great mathematical gifts, he was, according to Professor Olmsted, entitled to rank among the first astronomers of America, though he died the year after he graduated from Yale. Never a rugged person, his passion for astronomy, with its long night watchings, undoubtedly hastened his end. It was apparent to his family and friends before he finished college that he was suffering from consumption.

On leaving Nantucket, Ebenezer's father had become temporary pastor of a church in Collinsville, Connecticut, after which he took a small parish in Goshen, Massachusetts, near Ashfield, the native town of Alvan Clark. Ebenezer spent vacations with his family at both places, and in going to and coming from Goshen paid several

visits to Amasa Holcomb, the telescope maker of Southwick, Massachusetts, with whom he had carried on a frequent correspondence about telescopes. The telescope
which Ebenezer kept in his room during his freshman year
was a Holcomb instrument.

Amasa Holcomb, who was born at Granby, Connecticut,
June 18, 1787, was a forerunner of the Clarks in the
telescope trade. He made excellent instruments, and the
introduction of his telescopes is said to have marked an
era in astronomical science on this side of the Atlantic.
Although self-taught and having little knowledge of telescopes, he carried their manufacture to such perfection
that there was little need to import them from Europe.
The cheapness of his instruments made it possible for
many institutions and individuals, who otherwise could
not have afforded to buy a telescope, to equip themselves
with one. Holcomb's first attempt at grinding and polishing lenses was made about the year 1826. He had been
a schoolmaster and surveyor, and having several calls for
leveling instruments and not being able to procure easily
the small lenses for the eye pieces, he attempted to make
them himself. After a few trials he succeeded. About ten
years earlier, he had made a study of optics and knew
how lenses were ground in Europe, but he had no practical
experience. He had also studied astronomy and calculated
eclipses as early as 1806, and made observations on the
great eclipse of the sun that year. His success in grinding
and polishing lenses led him to try the construction of a
telescope. He first directed his attention to making refractors, such as the Clarks made later, and a few achro-
matics. Difficulty in procuring suitable glass, however,
discouraged him in making refractors, and he turned to

reflectors, with which he was so much more successful that he gave up the other kind altogether.

"When I commenced manufacturing telescopes," he said in 1842, "it was only with a view to my own gratification, without the least expectation of ever making it a business of profit. Some scientific men have, however, taken an interest in my success, and encouraged the sale. My telescopes are now in use in almost every state in the Union, and some have been ordered for foreign countries. I make them of any size required, but my manufacture is principally confined to the four following sizes and prices: the smallest size I make is 5 feet long, 4 inches aperture, with 4 eye-pieces, having powers from 40 to 300; mounted on a tripod stand, braced after the European manner—price $100. These will show the belts of Jupiter, the eclipses of his satellites, and such double stars as Castor, Herculis, Aquarii, 4 and 5 Lyrae. The next size is 7½ feet long, 6 inches aperture, with 5 eye-pieces, having powers from 40 to 600—price $250. With this size the division of Saturn's ring has been seen well defined all round, except that part behind the planet. The next size is 10 feet long, 8 inches aperture, with 6 eye-pieces, having powers from 100 to 1,000—price $600. The external work is plain, but substantial. All these, except the smallest, are mounted on a plan entirely my own. It is very simple; but for convenience and steadiness, I think it is not surpassed by any of those which are far more expensive. I have one of each size constantly on hand, so that I can furnish to any order without delay."

At the time Holcomb wrote this he had moved his telescope and spyglass works from Southwick to the adjoining town of Westfield, where, following the invention of the daguerreotype, he also made cameras. For many years he was an assessor of the town of Southwick, which he also represented in the legislature in 1832-33. From 1834 until his death in 1875 he was a justice of the peace.

Amasa Holcomb paid high tribute to the genius and attainments of his young friend, Ebenezer Porter Mason, when the boy astronomer died at the home of his aunt in Richmond, Virginia, December 26, 1840.

Tinkers

U NCLE SAM, with his starry blue swallowtail coat, his striped trousers, and stovepipe hat, has stood for the United States, as John Bull has symbolized Great Britain, for more than a century. His tall, spare figure, long, thin face, and scraggly chin whiskers are supposed to be typical of the New England countryman of the last century, and formerly he was always pictured indulging in the old Yankee pastime of whittling.

Whittling, indeed, was looked upon by foreigners as a peculiarly American characteristic, just as today gum-chewing is considered a conspicuous national trait. Americans, from elder statesmen to small boys, were invariably depicted with knife and shingle or clink of wood in hand. To foreign eyes, whittling appeared to be an idle, senseless habit, and was viewed with amused tolerance as a harmless foible of the American people. Actually, it was an instructive occupation, teaching mechanical dexterity

to youthful hands and stimulating the inventive faculties
of the mind.

"Why is it," asked a nineteenth-century New England
writer, "that we in the United States surpass all other
nations, in the excellence of our tools of all kinds? Why
are our axes, knives, hoes, spades, plows, the best in the
world? Because—in part, at least—we learn, in early
life, this alphabet of mechanics theoretical and practical—
whittling. Nearly every head and hand is trained t it.
We know and feel the difference between dull and sharp
tools. At ten years old, we are all epicures of cutting instruments."

Reverend John Pierpont, the New England lawyer and
father-in-law of J. Pierpont Morgan, who turned Unitar-
ian minister and at seventy-six went to the Civil War as
chaplain to a Massachusetts regiment, wrote a short poem
called "The Yankee Boy," in which the youthful urge to
whittle is humorously revealed.

> The Yankee boy before he's sent to school
> Well knows the mysteries of that magic tool,
> The pocket knife. For that his wistful eye
> Turns, while he hears his mother's lullaby;
> His hoarded cents he gladly gives to get it,
> Then leaves no stone unturned till he can whet it,
> And in the education of the lad
> No little part that implement hath had.

In Hartford, Connecticut, there is a statue of a young
sailor whittling industriously. It represents the youthful
Samuel Colt on shipboard, making the wooden model of
his first revolver, just as tradition says he did.

The Yankee mechanic, "forever contriving, planning,
whittling," has become a legendary figure. Whole volumes

Whittling

in folio are possible dealing with New England inventors
—Eli Whitney, Samuel F. B. Morse, Charles Goodyear,
and the rest—but here there is room only for brief
sketches of a few Yankee tinkers, who, though they may
not have altered the course of history, certainly enlivened
it.

The first is a son of Connecticut. If Abel Buell was a
fair sample of the population, Connecticut by no means
deserved to be called, as it was in earlier days, the Land
of Steady Habits. Buell was born at Killingworth in 1741
or 1742. He was apprenticed to a silversmith, but apparently got out of his time rather earlier than was good
for his undisciplined soul. He stuck out his shingle in
1762. Probably the silver- and goldsmithing business was
not very brisk in Killingworth, and he had time to think
up ways of bettering himself. One of the things that most
cried out for improvement was the Connecticut Colony
five-shilling note. Very little perspicacity was required to
see the advantage in notes for five pounds rather than five
shillings.

Making the alteration needed talents of a higher order,
but these, too, Buell possessed. He sat up nights improving
five-shilling notes into five-pound ones, thus richly earning
the description of "an uncommonly ingenious mechanic."
No one found anything to complain of in the new five-
pound notes—"They ought to be good, I made them myself," Buell might have said to his creditors. But the
neighbors did not think a boy of twenty, even though
married, could be up to any good when he kept a light
in his bedroom at all hours. Finally some local eaves-
dropper climbed a ladder to the window and thus spoiled
Buell's business without profiting his own.

The prosecutor was the king's attorney, Matthew Griswold, later a governor of Connecticut. Since Buell was young and had never been caught counterfeiting before, Griswold let him off as lightly as he could.

"Buell's punishment," says an early admirer, "appears to have consisted of imprisonment, *cropping* and *branding*. Only the tip of Buell's ear was cropped off: it was held on his tongue to keep it warm till it was put on the ear again, where it grew on. He was branded on the forehead as high up as possible. This was usually done by a hot iron, in the form of a letter designating the crime, which was held on the forehead of the criminal till he could say the words 'God save the king.' "

The imprisonment was neither long nor painful. Buell next invented and built the first lapidary machine used in this country, for cutting and polishing precious stones. "With this he was enabled to make a very curious ring; a large, beautiful stone being set in the center, surrounded by those of a smaller size, all of which were wrought in a curious and workmanlike manner. This ring he presented to Mr. Griswold, the king's attorney, and through his influence a pardon was obtained."

Buell's fame has been cherished largely by American printers, for it was he who first cut and cast type in the United States. Before his time the reading matter of the Colonies had been printed in chronically insufficient quantities of imported English and Dutch type, as it was also for some time after. Typefounding was not beyond the powers of so versatile a workman as Buell, and in May of 1769 the famous Boston shop of Edes & Gill printed an advertisement set in type that Buell had cut and cast. In October of that year the Connecticut Assembly gave Buell a subsidy of a hundred pounds, apparently not payable in Buell's homemade five-pound notes, to start a full-scale type foundry at New Haven. His old well-wisher Matthew Griswold had just been elected lieutenant governor.

Buell always preferred making new plans to toiling at old ones. For years the hundred pounds hung over him because he did nothing to earn it, and eventually his wife's exertions were what cleared off the debt. In 1770, when he should have been casting type, he started copperplate engraving. Three or four years later he engraved a chart of Saybrook Bar, which, despite its convivial sound, was merely intended to keep Connecticut riverboat skippers from running aground. When he finally got around to quantity type-casting, in 1781, another foundry was already going in Pennsylvania.

Buell's next claim to fame was in 1784. Right after the peace of 1783 he started work on a wall map, forty-one by forty-six inches, of the new United States. He compiled, engraved, and published it, producing the first map of the new political entity to be issued by one of its citizens.

It used to be supposed that Buell had some harum-scarum adventures in Florida while engraving Bernard Romans' charts of the Florida coast, and possibly he did. But he spent the last nineteen years of the eighteenth century largely in New Haven, and here his versatility quite ran away with him. He ran a packet-boat line, had an interest in a marble quarry, ran an auction business, either owned or shared in two privateersmen, made silver and jewelry, cast type, went on engraving, invented a cornplanter, and put on public show a Negro in the process of turning white.

In 1785 he invented a coining machine, with which—this time quite legally—he minted the copper money of

Connecticut for the next two or three years. It worked at the startling speed of two coppers per second.

The year of the French Revolution, 1789, saw him in England, learning about cotton manufacture. This was probably a month or two before Samuel Slater crossed the Atlantic the other way to put the American cotton business on its feet in Pawtucket. Buell's quick mind was no match for Slater's lifetime of experience. Although he worked at a cotton mill near New York in 1793, and built one of his own at New Haven in 1795, neither effort came to anything.

When Buell left New Haven for Hartford in 1799, he left inventing also behind him. He went on silversmithing and engraving, but we hear no more of his contraptions. In 1805 he went west—to Stockbridge, Massachusetts. For most of his life he had been a red-hot deist of the kind that quoted Tom Paine in barroom arguments; but in 1813 what old Timothy Dwight would have called an "interesting revival of religion" took place in western Massachusetts, and Abel caught it. He became a fiery Christian, and that is about the last I know of him until his death, which took place, with, I trust, proper Christian resignation, in the almshouse at New Haven in 1825.

Another of my favorite tinkers is Jacob Perkins, whose career paralleled Buell's in several ways, but whose character was as different as night from day. Born at Newburyport in 1766, he did not have the hard times of the Revolution to contend with in his own business. At the age of thirteen he was apprenticed, like Buell, to a goldsmith. His master died after three years, and Perkins carried on the business. The first of his many inventions was a better way of gold-plating shoe buckles. Then he, too, was called on to make coins. The state mint of Massachusetts, not yet superseded by federal coinage, employed twenty-one-year-old Perkins to engrave the dies for Massachusetts coppers.

Soon after this he invented a machine that would cut and head nails at one operation. He claimed it would produce two hundred thousand nails a day—faster work than heating each individual nail red-hot and beating it into shape, in the old way. The machine was splendid, but Perkins's business sense was not. He became involved with some irresponsible promoters, and went broke.

Perkins next concerned himself with the counterfeiting of paper money, only he was on the other side of the fence from Buell. He wanted to prevent it. A bill printed from type, or at most from a crude cut, could, as Buell had shown, be copied by any handy and ambitious youngster. The conventional method of preventing counterfeits was to deal very roughly with the counterfeiter if you caught him—which the memoirs of Stephen Burroughs and William Stewart lead us to think was very seldom. Perkins offered instead the revolutionary idea of making an engraved plate that could not be copied.

He called this the check-plate. It was composite, made of many small, square steel bars set up on end and locked together. On the smooth surface formed by the ends of the bars he engraved a complicated overall pattern. Then he unlocked the bars, turned them every which way, and locked them together again in their new positions. The disjointed parts of the old design formed an irrational new pattern quite impossible to copy in the days before photoengraving.

In connection with the check-plate Perkins made a discovery that brought a new era in illustration. He learned how to decarbonize or soften steel and harden it again

at will. In that way he could engrave on a steel plate de-
signs even more delicate than he could on copper, and
afterward harden the plate so that it would print an in-
definite number of impressions. All the elegantly illustrated, tombstone-sized volumes that weighed down your
grandfather's parlor table owed their adornment to Perkins's invention. By playing his tricks with hard and soft
steel, Perkins could transfer a design from one plate to
another, or from a plate to a roller, and so make as many
copies of a literally inimitable check-plate as he needed.
Steel cylinders made by his method also found wide use
in calico printing.

Around 1809, Massachusetts passed a law requiring
banks to use check-plates on their bills. The Bank of
England, however, still muddled through with the old
copper plates, and so had to keep hanging an endless
crop of counterfeiters. This was apparently costly in
legal expenses, because the bank offered a thousand-pound
prize for a good way to stop counterfeiting.

Perkins had spent several years in the commercial
metropolis of Philadelphia, where he met another Yankee
engraver, Gideon Fairman of Newtown, Connecticut.

In 1818 Perkins went to London in search of the bank's
thousand-pound prize. The bank, although it could find
no flaws in Perkins's check-plate scheme, was not going
to shell out a thousand quid to a damned Yankee. Executing counterfeiters was the lesser of two evils.

Nevertheless Perkins stayed in London and went into
the steelplate printing business with Gideon Fairman. The
business they started is still going. It printed the first
penny-postage stamp for Sir Rowland Hill. "Few have
done more to raise the fame of American ingenuity
abroad," says an early industrial historian.

Possibly Perkins had a rough voyage over. At any rate, this or something else led him to doubt the ancient idea that water was incompressible. The belief is true enough for all practical purposes, as any inexpert swandiver can testify, but it is not a fact of physics. Perkins was among the first to suspect this, and he was *the* first to prove it. He next invented the bathometer, which I used to suppose was a thermometer for the tub but have since discovered measures the depth of sea water, and also a meter for measuring the relative speeds of a boat through the water.

From sea water to steam was a natural enough step. Perkins worked on high-pressure steam generation, a field in which his son Angier March Perkins and his grandson Loftus Perkins later became eminent, and invented a steam cannon. Though the cannon never got to war—it was too complicated—the Iron Duke in person watched a trial of it in England.

Perkins retired in 1834, and died in 1849.

It is impossible for me to think of Yankee mechanics without thinking of Eli Terry, who is so greatly revered by clock collectors. He was born in 1722 at East Windsor, Connecticut, not far from his unfortunate fellow-clockmaker John Fitch, of steamboat fame, who, however, disliked clockmaking nearly as much as Bronson Alcott later disliked work in the factory of Terry's partner. He was apprenticed to a very competent clockmaker named Burnap, who taught him to make both brass and wooden clockworks, and to engrave the dials. Incidentally, the great engraver-historian John Warner Barber also came from East Windsor, but after Terry's time.

Terry came out of his apprenticeship at a turning point in American clockmaking. He knew how to go through every step in building a clock, from constructing his own tools and casting brass wheels to engraving flourishes on the face. All household clock movements were made for the tall cases we call grandfather clocks. The best movements were made of brass, with a brass dial; cheaper ones had wooden wheels, but a dial also of brass.

Before Terry got out of his time, in 1792, most clockmakers were already buying their brass wheels from a Hartford foundry. The old skilled craft was becoming an assembly job. One might have supposed that this would give people ideas about mass production. In clockmaking, however, that innovation was reserved for young Eli. In 1793 he moved from East Windsor to what was about to become Plymouth, Connecticut. He made brass and wooden tall clocks, repaired watches, and retailed spectacles. He married in 1795, and set up housekeeping with household furniture consisting, we are told, of two chairs, two cups, and two saucers. He was still just a young country clockmaker making an occasional clock when he could get an order.

Then, about 1802, he started using water power to produce the wheels for wooden clockworks, and took a couple of lads to help him. Like many a manufacturer since, he now found he had set production and sales to driving each other alternately. There was not a living in brass-wheeled clocks made to order, so he began producing wooden-wheeled ones for stock. Only then he had to go out and peddle the stock.

Clockmakers in Terry's youth generally sold just the works, hands, dial, pendulum, and weights of a clock. The customer went out and hired a cabinetmaker to build as good a case as he could afford; or else he simply hung up the works uncased as a "wag-on-the-wall." Without the cases and weights, Terry could pack four clocks around his saddle on horseback, at the four points of the compass. He went over into wild territory, sometimes even beyond the Hudson, and sold his clocks to civilization-hungry new settlers.

The selling was easy, the collecting not so easy. Theoretically he got twenty-five dollars for a clock; more often it would be two saddlebags full of salt pork. He also learned before long that taking his customers' notes of hand, though frequently necessary, was invariably risky. Terry and other peddling clockmakers from Hartford and Litchfield counties infested all the less cultivated country within reach on horseback, and soon made the buying public acutely conscious of wooden-wheeled clocks. Probably Terry himself had no idea then of the market that was building up.

The market, of course, was the trick. Eli Whitney had known beforehand that army rifles would always be wanted. In 1798 he contracted with the United States government to make ten thousand muskets, and he set out to do it by the system of interchangeable manufacture— any part from one rifle would fit perfectly into any other rifle. Whitney expected to do the job in a year but actually took ten. He had not finished his contract when two brothers in Waterbury offered a similar one, for clocks, to Eli Terry.

No one knows for sure that Terry got the idea of interchangeable manufacture straight from Whitney, but there are hints to that effect. Certainly without the interchangeable system Terry could not have undertaken to produce four thousand wooden clock movements with hands and dials in three years. Plenty of people said the brothers in Waterbury were crazy to want such a thing anyway. The brothers supplied Terry with the stock, and Terry was to hand it back in the shape of clocks at four dollars per clock. Terry's operation was, of course, cheaper and altogether easier than Whitney's; even so, he was entitled to be quite pleased with himself for finishing a thousand clocks the second year of his contract, and the other three thousand the third year.

From that time on Terry, without bestriding a horse, could sell his wooden-wheeled clocks faster than he could make them. The real growth came after 1814, when he invented a shelf clock, complete with a case about two feet high, so that you no longer had to hire a cabinetmaker. He took in as partners two of his workmen, Seth Thomas and Silas Hoadley, but within a short time they found there was business enough for everyone, and set up independently. Seth Thomas, originally a joiner who built cases for the shelf clocks, was in some ways the least remarkable of the three; his firm, however, is the only one still in business under the founder's name.

Once Terry had shown how to make cheap clocks, all the wooden-nutmeg artists in Connecticut turned their ingenuity to selling them. The Connecticut clock business grew into a veritable South Sea bubble. You can easily look at two dozen Connecticut wooden clocks without finding the same maker twice. Another of Eli Terry's young men, Chauncey Jerome, went into the clock business with P. T. Barnum, and each blamed the other when both went broke.

Eli Terry, with the solidity of an earlier Connecticut in his character, avoided this peril. He took his son Eli, Jr., into the business, and in 1833 retired on an income of three thousand dollars a year—more money than he had known there was in the world twenty-five years before. I

have always liked the explanation he gave for his success
in life. He did not ascribe it to hard work, economy, and
temperance, though he was a shining example of all three;
he said it was his son Eli, Jr., who often had courage to
go on when he himself would have despaired.

In 1826 Eli, Sr., stirred up the town of New Haven
with a clock that he installed in the steeple of Centre
Church. This clock, like all clocks nowadays, kept mean
time. That is, it showed an hour whose length was determined by dividing the year into 8,760 equal parts. The
good people of New Haven, however, led by a God-fear-
ing Yale College, still kept sun time, and Terry's mean
time threw them off their stroke; they thought it mean by
name and mean by nature. The fact that Terry had ingen-
iously contrived the clock to show both mean and sun time
did not reconcile the class of people who a century later
upheld God's time against daylight-saving. For months
the New Haven newspapers echoed with snappish com-
ments and rejoinders. Eventually it seems to have been
a drawn battle. The clock stayed in the steeple, and the
more fervid Congregationalists maintained their right to
sniff at it and do business by the noon mark on the win-
dowsill.

Eli, Sr., got out of the wooden-clock business just
about in time. The Ives brothers in Bristol, the next town
to Plymouth, invented a clock made out of rolled brass instead of the old-fashioned cast brass. It was just as cheap
to make as a wooden-wheeled clock and did not swell up
and stop in wet weather. Besides, the panic of 1837 soured
everyone on boom businesses; many of the newcomers
were shaken out of clockmaking.

Eli, Jr., weathered the storm and made both wooden
and brass clocks; but he died in 1841, a decade before his

father, and without him his firm soon failed. Though Eli, Sr., went on building fine timekeepers for his own amusement, he left business worries to his other sons and grandsons.

Clockmaking no longer dominates the industry of central Connecticut, but the products that do are all direct offshoots of clock manufacture. Sheet brass, ball bearings, and locks all struck root in Plymouth and Bristol either because Terry's successors needed them or because the new factories needed something that the clock industry produced. The New Departure ball-bearing concern, for one, began by making patent doorbells that required the springs and cogwheels so abundant in Bristol; from doorbells to bicycle coaster-brakes and thence to ball bearings was an easy shift.

For a Connecticut man, Terry cared remarkably little about money. Even less mercenary was Samuel Morey, ten years his senior, who was born at Hebron, Connecticut, in 1762. When he was four his family moved way up into the wilderness of Orford, New Hampshire, and the rest of his life was spent on the stretch of the Connecticut River between Orford and Fairlee, Vermont.

Terry never took any interest in machinery unconnected with clocks; Morey held twenty-one American patents for everything from a steam-driven roasting spit to a windmill water-pump. He lived comfortably on the income from a sawmill and invented because he could not leave inventing alone.

Oddly enough, his greatest practical achievement—a reliable, working steamboat—was his first. He ran a boat on Fairlee Pond in 1790, and by 1792 he had it going upstream in the Connecticut River at four and a half miles an hour. His first patent, however, was for the steam spit, in January of 1793. The steamboat patent did not come until 1795.

John Fitch, the ex-clockmaker, Oliver Evans, and James Rumsey apparently contrived to move small boats by steam power a couple of years before Morey, and of course long before Fulton; but barely moving was about all their vessels would do. Morey steered his own craft up and down the Connecticut at will. He took his first trial runs in 1793 on Sundays, so that people would be at meeting and not gaping along the river bank. Then he captained his vessel from Hartford, Connecticut, to New York, sustaining better than five miles an hour. In all his public steamboating career, Morey never had an accident or breakdown. The bankruptcy of a principal backer in Bordentown, New Jersey, was what kept him from establishing the first regular steamboat line.

Morey had a lot of trouble with Fulton and Fulton's backer, Robert Livingstone. In the end Fulton's party launched commercial steam navigation, building mostly on Morey's patents. I say patents because, out of the twenty-one he held, five applied to steam engines. Most of the rest covered other kinds of engines or methods of heating. I feel that too little attention has been devoted to the widespread infringement of his patent signed by James Madison and James Monroe on April 8, 1812: "A unique and efficient method for the use of hot air as power." He might have done better with a patent for its prevention.

Morey's next-to-last patent was signed on April Fool's Day, 1826, by John Quincy Adams and Henry Clay. Who was the victim of the joke I am not quite sure. It covered an internal combustion engine run on water and spirits of turpentine. Puzzle: was he the April Fool because he did not popularize his machine, or are we, because someone else did?

Morey was a true Yankee character, but not of the spiny kind. He used to boast that he had never been sued or gone to law, which was quite an achievement when his friends were waging a running battle with Fulton and Livingstone. He went on placidly playing with steamboats in his retirement long after Fulton had hogged the credit. Once when there was a particularly attractive public hanging at Haverhill, New Hampshire, he organized an all-day picnic to keep the small boys of Fairlee away from it, and the boys remembered long afterward that the outing had been "more fun than a hanging."

His own idea of fun, after he moved to Fairlee Pond (since rechristened Lake Morey), was to study the behavior of the fish in the pond; in the end he became something of an ichthyologist. And for all his mildness about profits, his biographer, George Calvin Carter, observes that, "At the time of his death he owned four houses, the Fish House on the lake, a houseboat on the lake, a treadmill with side paddle wheels, what was then the most modern and efficient sawmill in New England, and 3,400 acres of fine virgin timber, all free from indebtedness of any kind."

Morey's most spectacular living monument is the beautiful row of white houses on the ridge at Orford. He built the first two, one for himself and one for his daughter on her marriage. The Orford houses include the only samples of Bulfinch domestic architecture known outside Boston, and some people think the green has no equal anywhere in New England.

Female Defenders

PRESENCE of mind and bravery in the face of danger were common traits of the pioneer women of New England. Quite apart from the ordinary hazards and hardships of frontier life, there was always the suspense and dread of Indian depredations. Even the periods between open hostilities were seasons of desultory mischief. The settlers in the wilderness lived in an environment that was seldom anything but terrifying, especially for the women and children. Sometimes in an emergency the women showed themselves more resourceful than the men. Here, for example, is an instance of female prowess deserving of remembrance.

A party of Narragansett Indians who had been hunting on the outskirts of Dorchester, Massachusetts, called at the house of Mr. Minot and demanded food and drink. When this was refused, they left, showing marked signs of resentment, and their sachem swore vengeance. One of the band, named Chicataubutt, who remained behind for this purpose, concealed himself in the underbrush near the house. The following morning he saw Mr. and Mrs. Minot depart for Boston. The Minots left their two children in the care of a servant girl, with strict instructions to remain in the house and under no circumstances to open the door to anyone until their return. Shortly after they had gone, the girl saw Chicataubutt approaching the house. Looking about to make sure no one was around, he made a sudden rush for the door, only to find it barred. Undeterred by this, he tried to get in through the window, but the young woman was ready for him. She had hidden the children under two brass kettles, bidding them not to stir or make the slightest noise. She had then taken down and loaded a musket belonging to the household. Seeing that she was armed, the savage fired at her through the window but missed, whereupon she shot him through the shoulder. This, however, did not stop him, and as he persisted in trying to enter the room through the window, she threw a shovelful of live coals in his face, most of which lodged in his blanket. This was too hot a reception for the Indian, and in terrible agony from the red-hot brands he fled and the next day was found dead in the woods.

News of the brave stand made by the girl reached the government of Massachusetts Bay, and she was officially honored by the present of a silver wristband engraved with her name and the words, "She slew the Narragansett hunter."

In another case an Indian tried to enter a house defended by a lone woman by descending, Santa Claus fashion, down the chimney, but, sensing the direction from which the attack was coming, the plucky woman threw a mattress filled with corn husks on the embers in the fireplace and gave the Indian a good roasting before he could escape back up the chimney.

At dawn on August 29, 1708, a party of two hundred and fifty French and Indians fell upon the town of Haverhill, Massachusetts, killing and capturing about forty of the inhabitants and burning and plundering a large part of the town. In this desperate situation the women of Haverhill displayed great heroism.

The first house attacked was that of the Reverend Benjamin Rolfe. Awakened by shots and outcries, Mr. Rolfe sprang from his bed and, placing himself against the door which the savages were attempting to break in, he called upon the three soldiers quartered in his house for assistance; but the soldiers were paralyzed with fear and did nothing to help defend the place. The Indians, failing to break down the door, fired two shots through it, wounding Mr. Rolfe in the elbow, and then renewed the assault. Finding that he could not hold them back any longer, the minister fled through the house and out the back door but was overtaken and butchered near his well. Returning to the house, the Indians found Mrs. Rolfe with her infant child, Mehitabel, in her arms and killed them both. As for the three cowardly soldiers, they begged the hatchet men in vain for their lives, and their bodies were counted among the promiscuous dead.

Two of the Rolfe children were saved by the presence of mind and courage of a colored woman named Hagar, a slave belonging to the Rolfe family. Jumping from her bed at the first alarm, she carried to the cellar the two girls, aged six and eight, and, covering each with a tub, hid herself. The Indians in search of plunder entered the cellar, and although they repeatedly passed the tubs concealing the children, even stepping on the foot of one, they did not find them. Nor did they discover Hagar hiding behind a meat barrel from which they helped themselves. Another inmate of the household, Ann Whittaker, escaped by jumping into an apple chest under the stairs, where she remained undetected. These particular Indians do not seem to have been very good at the game of hide-and-seek.

Another party of Indians went to the home of Captain Simon Wainwright, commander of the militia, killing him at the first shot. Mrs. Wainwright, exhibiting no fear whatsoever, unbarred the door and admitted the Indians. She greeted them cordially, waited on them with alacrity, and promised to get them whatever they wanted. The Indians were nonplused by their cheerful reception and kindly treatment when they had expected just the opposite. At length, however, they did demand money from her, and Mrs. Wainwright, retiring to get it, took the opportunity to escape with all her children, save one daughter, who was taken prisoner.

There were three soldiers quartered in the Wainwright house, who, while Mrs. Wainwright parleyed with the Indians, barricaded themselves in the upstairs rooms. They were not cowards like those at the Rolfe home, and stood ready to defend themselves to the end. When the Indians realized how completely Mrs. Wainwright had fooled them, they attacked the soldiers furiously but met with such stout resistance that finally, after attempting to set fire to the house, they withdrew. Two Indians skulking outside the house were killed by the soldiers.

Mr. and Mrs. Swan, who lived in a house in a field, saw two Indians approaching and decided to fight for their own and their children's lives. The door of their house was so narrow that only one person at a time could enter. Mr. and Mrs. Swan held the door as the Indians threw themselves against it. Unable to open it in this way, one of the Indians stood with his back to it and pushed while the other pressed against him. The husky warriors were more than a match for the Swans and were slowly opening the door when Mr. Swan, who is said to have been a rather timid man, suggested to his wife that perhaps the best thing to do was to let them in, but she wouldn't hear of it. As the leading Indian was crowding in past the door, Mrs. Swan seized her iron spit, which was nearly a yard long, and summoning all her strength drove it clear through the savage's body. This proved so discouraging to the attackers that they gave up the contest and went away. It was undoubtedly the fighting spirit of Mrs. Swan that saved the family.

This attack on Haverhill was by no means the only time the inhabitants had experienced the horrors of Indian warfare, nor the first time the women of the town had shown their valor. Haverhill was the home of the famous Mrs. Hannah Dustin, who a little more than a decade before had been taken by the Indians but returned in triumph from her captivity with ten Indian scalps—trophies which won her the New England women's championship. The best account of Mrs. Dustin's remarkable adventure is in Mirrick's *History of Haverhill* (1832), an account that is too good to spoil by rewriting, though here it is necessarily presented in somewhat abridged form.

"On the 15th of March, 1697, a body of Indians made a descent on the westerly part of the town, and approached the house of Mr. Thomas Dustin. Mr. Dustin at this time was engaged abroad in his daily labor. When the terrific shouts of the blood-hounds first fell on his ear, he seized his gun, mounted his horse, and hastened to his house, with the hope of escorting to a place of safety his family, which consisted of his wife, who had been confined only seven days in childbed, her nurse, Mrs. Mary Neff, and eight young children. He instantly ordered seven of his children to fly in an opposite direction from that in which the danger was approaching, and went himself to assist his wife. But he was too late—before she could arise from her bed, the enemy were upon them.

"Mr. Dustin, seeing there was no hope of saving his wife from the clutches of the foe, flew from the house, mounted his horse, and rode full speed after his flying children. The agonized father supposed it impossible to save them all, and he determined to snatch from death the child which shared the most of his affections. He gazed upon them, and faltered in his resolution, for there was none whom he could leave behind. He resolved to defend them from the murderers, or die at their side.

"A small party of the Indians pursued Mr. Dustin as he fled from the house, and soon overtook him and his flying children. They did not, however, approach very near, for they saw his determination, and feared the vengeance of a father, but skulked behind the trees and fences, and fired upon him and his little company. Mr. Dustin dismounted from his horse, placed himself in the rear of his children, and returned the fire of the enemy often and with good success. In this manner he retreated for more than a mile, alternately encouraging his terrified charges, and loading and firing his gun, until he lodged them safely in a fortified house. The Indians, finding that they could not conquer him, returned to their companions, expecting, no doubt, that they should there find victims, on which they might exercise their savage cruelty.

"The party which entered the house when Mr. Dustin left it, found Mrs. Dustin in bed, and the nurse attempting to fly with the infant in her arms. They ordered Mrs.

Dustin to rise instantly, while one of them took the infant from the arms of the nurse, carried it out, and dashed out its brains against an apple tree. After plundering the house they set it on fire, and commenced their retreat,

Escape of the Dustin family

though Mrs. Dustin had but partly dressed herself, and was without a shoe on one of her feet. The weather at the time was exceedingly cold, the March wind blew keen and piercing, and the earth was alternately covered with snow and deep mud.

"They travelled twelve miles the first day, and continued their retreat, day by day, following a circuitous route, until they reached the home of the Indian who claimed them as his property, which was on a small island, now called Dustin's Island, at the mouth of the Contoocook river, about six miles above the state house in Concord, New Hampshire. Notwithstanding their intense suffering for the death of the child—their anxiety for those whom they had left behind, and who they expected had been cruelly butchered—their sufferings from cold and hunger, and from sleeping on the damp earth, with nothing but an inclement sky for a covering—and their terror for themselves, lest the arm that, as they supposed, had slaughtered those whom they dearly loved, would soon be made red with their blood,—notwithstanding all this, they performed the journey without yielding, and arrived at their destination in comparative health."

There were twelve Indians in the party—two men, three women, and seven children, besides an English boy named Samuel Lennardson, who about a year before had been taken prisoner at Worcester.

"These unfortunate women had been but a few days with the Indians, when they were informed that they must soon start for a distant Indian settlement, and that, upon their arrival, they would be obliged to conform to the regulations always required of prisoners, whenever they entered the village, which was, to be stripped, scourged, and run the gantlet in a state of nudity. Soon as the two women were informed of this, they determined to escape as speedily as possible. They could not bear to be exposed to the scoffs and unrestrained gaze of their savage conquerors—death would be preferable. Mrs. Dustin soon planned a mode of escape, appointed the 31st inst. for its accomplishment, and prevailed upon her nurse and the boy to join her. The Indians kept no watch, for the boy had lived with them so long they considered him as one of their children, and they did not expect that the women, inadvised and unaided, would attempt to escape, when success, at the best, appeared so desperate."

The day before Mrs. Dustin asked the boy to find out from one of the men where they hit their victims when they wished to kill them quickly. "Strike him there," said the Indian, laying a finger on his temple. He then instructed him in the art of scalping. The boy passed this information on to Mrs. Dustin.

"The night at length arrived, and the whole family retired to rest, little suspecting that the most of them would never behold another sun. Long before the break of day, Mrs. Dustin arose, and, having ascertained that they were all in a deep sleep, awoke her nurse and the boy, when they armed themselves with tomahawks, and despatched ten of the twelve. A favorite boy they designedly left; and one of the squaws, whom they left for dead, jumped up and ran with him into the woods. Mrs. Dustin killed her master, and Samuel Lennardson despatched the very Indian who told him where to strike, and how to take off a scalp. The deed was accomplished before the day began to break, and after securing what little provision the wigwam of their dead master afforded, they scuttled all the boats but one, to prevent pursuit, and with that started for their homes. Mrs. Dustin took with her a gun that belonged to her master, and the tomahawk with which she committed the tragical deed. They had not proceeded far, however, when Mrs. Dustin perceived that they had neglected to take their scalps, and feared that her neighbors, if they ever arrived at their homes, would not credit their story, and would ask them for some token or proof. She told her fears to her companions, and they immediately returned to the silent wigwam, took off the scalps of the fallen, and put them into a bag. They then started on their journey anew, with the gun, tomahawk, and the bleeding trophies,—palpable witnesses of their heroic and unparalleled deed.

"A long and weary journey was before them, but they commenced it with cheerful hearts, each alternately rowing and steering their little bark. Though they had escaped from the clutches of their unfeeling master, still they were surrounded with dangers. They were thinly clad, the sky was still inclement, and they were liable to be recaptured by strolling bands of Indians, or by those who would undoubtedly pursue them so soon as the squaw and the boy had reported their departure, and the terrible vengeance they had taken; and were they again made prisoners, they well knew that a speedy death would follow. This array of danger, however, did not appall them, for home was their beacon-light, and the thoughts of their firesides nerved their hearts. They continued to drop silently down the river, keeping a good lookout for strolling Indians; and in the night two of them only slept, while the third managed the boat. In this manner they pursued their journey, until they arrived safely, with their trophies, at their homes, totally unexpected by their mourning friends, who supposed that they had been butchered by their ruthless conquerors.

"After recovering from the fatigue of the journey, they started for Boston, where they arrived on the 21st of April. They carried with them the gun and tomahawk, and their ten scalps—those witnesses that would not lie; and while there, the General Court gave them fifty pounds, as a reward for their heroism. The report of their daring deed soon spread into every part of the country, and when Colonel Nicholson, governor of Maryland, heard of it, he sent them a very valuable present, and many presents were also made to them by their neighbors."

There were some people who criticized Mrs. Dustin for her massacre of the Indians, particularly the slaying of the Indian children, but far worse was the terrible vengeance taken by the fishwives of Marblehead, near Boston, against two helpless Indian prisoners in that town. Increase Mather mentions it in a letter written in 1677 to Mr. Cotton: "Sabbath-day was sennight, the women of Marblehead, as they came out of the meeting-house, fell upon two Indians that were brought in as captives, and, in a tumultuous way, barbarously murdered them. Doubtless, if the Indians hear of it, the captives among them will be served accordingly."

Terrible, indeed, were the experiences of many of the women who underwent captivity by the Indians. If on the long trek to Canada, where the captives were sold, they could not keep up with the rest, they were given their quietus beside the trail with a tomahawk and their bodies left for birds and beasts to feed upon. But concerning one thing they never had to worry. The Indians never took toll of their women prisoners. President Dwight of Yale College said, "It ought to be observed to the immortal honor of these people, distinguished as they are by so many traits of brutal ferocity, that history records no instance in which the purity of a female captive was violated by them, or even threatened."

This remarkable continence by the American savages puzzled and interested President Dwight. Europeans, he said, attributed it to a frosty insensibility of constitution. President Dwight admitted that the Indian manner of living was certainly such as might prevent the intenseness of sensual passion which is the result of the stimulating power of luxury, but he was not prepared to accept this as the correct explanation, and began to ask questions of those who were intimately acquainted with the character and manners of the Indians.

"The Hon. Timothy Edwards, a Commissioner of Indian Affairs," he wrote, "informed me that this specimen of Indian moderation was not derived at all from the want of sexual passion, but from a very different source. He observed that after the Indian youth have grown to such years, as enable them to comprehend and feel the full import of such instruction, the old men going round from house to house enjoin upon them abstinence in the most solemn and forceful manner. 'Remember,' they customarily say to these objects of their care 'that you are men; that if you behave as you ought, you may expect to be hunters, and renowned warriors. Your proper business is to acquire glory. You are to pursue the deer; and to vanquish the wolf, the bear, and the catamount. You are to uphold the honor of your nation; to subdue its enemies; and to return home from war, loaded with spoils, and crowned with victory. The old men are to point you out as heroes; and the virgins are to sing your praises. Yield not yourselves then to weak silly contemptible passions, which will change you into women. However beautiful your captives may be, look not at them. They will corrupt, debase, and destroy you. Your glory will wither; you will lose the name of men. Your fathers did not thus. They scaled the mountains to chase the bear, and the scalps of their enemies adorned their weekwams. Follow their steps; be men; and let your names go down to future generations as theirs have come down to you.' "

President Dwight thought that this injunction reiterated at the most susceptible period of life by men of the first distinction in the tribe furnished the true explanation of the remarkable fact mentioned.

There were, of course, cases of miscegenation, of white women going native and marrying Indians, the result more often than not of capture and long residence among the redskins. White children taken when very young and brought up by the Indians sometimes remained with them for life. But, on the whole, the women of Colonial New England had little use for the savages.

Hermits

Hermits as a rule do not propagate, but New England has always had its share of these curiosities, who have generally been viewed by the people with interest and tolerance. New England can even boast of that rare occurrence—a lady hermit. This was Sarah Bishop, who lived for many years at Ridgefield, Connecticut, and concerning whom Samuel G. Goodrich wrote the following account in his *Recollections of a Lifetime* (1856). It is a most extraordinary picture.

"Sarah Bishop was, at the period of my boyhood, a thin, ghostly old woman, bent and wrinkled, but still possessing a good deal of activity. She lived in a cave, formed by nature, in a mass of projecting rocks that overhung a deep valley or gorge in West Mountain. This was about four miles from our house, and was, I believe, actually within the limits of North Salem; but being on the eastern side of the mountain, it was most easily accessible from Ridgefield, and hence its tenant was called an inhabitant of our town.

"This strange woman was no mere amateur recluse. The rock—bare and desolate—was actually her home, except that occasionally she strayed to the neighborhood villages, seldom being absent more than one or two days at a time. She never begged, but received such articles as were given to her. She was of a highly religious turn of mind, and at long intervals came to our church, and partook of the sacrament. She sometimes visited our family —the only one thus favored in the town—and occasionally remained over night. She never would eat with us at the table, nor engage in general conversation. Upon her early history she was invariably silent; indeed, she spoke of her affairs with great reluctance. She neither seemed to have sympathy for others, nor to ask it in return. If there was any exception, it was only in respect to the religious exercises of the family: she listened intently to the reading of the Bible, and joined with apparent devotion in the morning and evening prayer. . . ."

"In my rambles among the mountains," Mr. Goodrich continues, "I have seen her passing through the forest, or sitting silent as a statue upon the prostrate trunk of a tree, or perchance upon a stone or mound, scarcely to be distinguished from the inanimate objects—wood, earth, and rock—around her. She had a sense of propriety as to personal appearance, for when she visited the town, she was decently, though poorly, clad; when alone in the wilderness she seemed little more than a squalid mass of rags. My excursions frequently brought me within the wild precincts of her solitary den. Several times I have paid a visit to the spot, and in two instances found her at home.

"A place more desolate—in its general outline—more

absolutely given up to the wildness of nature, it is impossible to conceive. Her cave was a hollow in the rock, about six feet square. Except a few rags and an old basin, it was without furniture—her bed being the floor of the cave, and her pillow a projecting point of the rock. It was entered by a natural door about three feet wide and four feet high, and was closed in severe weather only by pieces of bark. At a distance of a few feet was a cleft, where she kept a supply of roots and nuts, which she gathered, and the food that was given her. She was reputed to have a secret depository, where she kept a quantity of antique dresses, several of them of rich silks, and apparently suited to a fashionable life: though I think this was an exaggeration. At a little distance down the ledge, there was a fine spring of water, in the vicinity of which she was often found in fair weather. . . .

"A place at once so secluded and so wild was, of course, the chosen haunt of birds, beasts, and reptiles. The eagle built her nest and reared her young in the clefts of the rocks; foxes found shelter in the caverns, and serpents reveled alike in the dry hollows of the cliffs, and the dank recesses of the valley. The hermitess had made companionship with these brute tenants of the wood. The birds had become so familiar with her, that they seemed to heed her almost as little as if she had been a stone. The fox fearlessly pursued his hunt and his gambols in her presence. The rattlesnake hushed his monitory signal as he approached her. Such things, at least, were entertained by the popular belief. It was said, indeed, that she had domesticated a particular rattlesnake, and that he paid her daily visits. She was accustomed—so said the legend—to bring him milk from the villages, which he devoured with great relish. . . .

The Hermitess of Ridgefield

"The early history of this strange personage was involved in some mystery. So much of this, however, was ascertained, that she was of good family, and had lived on Long Island. During the Revolutionary War—in one of the numerous forays of the British soldiers—her father's house was burned; and, as if this were not enough, she was made the victim of one of those demoniacal acts, which in peace are compensated by the gibbet, but which, in war, embellish the life of the soldier. Desolate in fortune, blighted at heart, she fled from human society, and for a long time concealed her sorrows in the cavern which she had accidentally found. Her grief—softened by time, perhaps alleviated by a veil of insanity—was at length so far mitigated, that, although she did not seek human society, she could endure it."

Sarah Bishop, the Nun of the Mountain, continued to occupy her cave until 1810 or 1811. She had gradually become more bent, her limbs more thin and wasted, her hair more blanched, her eyes more colorless. When spring came and she was not seen in any of the neighboring villages, some of the inhabitants went to the mountain, where they found the hermitess dead.

A contemporary of Sarah Bishop was a hermit named Timothy Learned, who lived in the town of New Marlborough, in the hilly region of southwestern Massachusetts, an account of whom appeared in the *Connecticut Courant* at the time of the recluse's death. Like Thoreau, Timothy Learned lived beside a pond, which for many years was known as Hermit Pond but is now called East India Pond.

"Timothy Learned died in New Marlborough in 1817, aged seventy. He was born near Canterbury, in Connecticut, of parents in low circumstances, and bound out and

brought up in Woodbury. After he was of age, he went
to the town of Fredericksburgh (N. Y.) where his father
then resided. When he was twenty-four, he came into this
town, a sprightly and industrious young man. He purchased a lot of new land remote from any settlement; went
to work, cleared a fine piece of land, and, with the help of
his brother, who afterwards came to him, erected a small
log-house, in which they lived together harmoniously.
After a year and a half he visited his friends, and returned
a perfect misanthrope; was displeased and quarreled with
his brother, and drove him away. He gradually became
deranged. During the Revolution he fancied himself commander-in-chief, and frequently gave orders for the regu-
lation of Congress and the army, copies of which are
now to be seen. He called himself admiral. He became
troublesome and dangerous, and was disarmed by the civil
authority.

"Since that time he has sought no intercourse with the
rest of the world; has lived alone in the wilderness, and
obtained his subsistence by the cultivation of not more than
an acre of land. This he manured with grass, leaves, potatoes, and pumpkins. For a time he kept some stock; had
some pasture; but for a number of years he has lived
alone, with the exception of a few domesticated fowls.
Woodchucks, rabbits, skunks, weasels, squirrels, rats, and
mice, and these without dressing, were the varieties of his
table. His clothing consisted of two garments, fastened
together at the waist by large wooden pins, and was made
of wool, hemp, or flax, twisted coarse, and wove in narrow stripes, sewed together, and put on and worn out,
probably, without cleansing, and shoes, or moccasins of
bark shaped to his feet and worn off. He could read, always
kept the year, day of the month, and week. He was not dis-

posed to converse much on religious subjects. He, however, kept a Testament; paid some regard to the Sabbath; was addicted somewhat to profanity, and was a lover of ardent spirits. He expected after death to be about and take some care of his farm.

"For some years his strength had been failing, but he kept about till the very day before he died. His friends have endeavored to draw him from his retirement, but in vain. Thousands from the neighboring towns have visited the hermit, for so he was called. He has often in the summer season been found naked, his head uncovered and uncombed, and his beard unshaven. His neighbors have been disposed to assist him, but he has generally rejected their offers. The night on which he died, though his dress was uncomfortable and filthy, finding him very weak, they wished to have remained with him; but no, tomorrow he should be about again. But in the morning early he was found a corpse. His remains were the next day committed, with suitable religious services, and in the presence of a large concourse, to the dust, on the place where he had spent almost half a century in the manner described."

A note in Dwight's *Travels in New England and New York* (1821) tells of a New Hampshire hermit, a grubby character who lived near Portsmouth and always spoke of the town by its ancient name of Strawberry Bank. The note, which is in the form of an obituary notice written at the time of the solitaire's death, is attributed to a local clergyman.

"Died, at Sagamore Creek, on Friday morning, the 17th, Mr. Benjamin Lear, eighty-two years of age, and was interred the following day on his own land.

"It is presumed, that no man ever died, within the limits of Portsmouth, who deserved the name of hermit more than Mr. Lear.

"The farm, on which he lived, and which he owned, was of sufficient extent and fertility to have supported a large family; but he had long imbibed the idea, that he should live to need and spend the whole.

"For more than twenty years he dwelt entirely alone in a hut, which scarcely anyone would have deemed decent for a barn. He made his own garments, which were in a fashion peculiar to himself. He tilled his land, milked his cows, and made his butter and cheese; but subsisted principally on potatoes and milk. Owing, no doubt, to his simple and temperate mode of living, he exhibited, at the age of eighty-two, a face freer from wrinkles than is generally seen in those of fifty. . . .

"Mr. Lear, although repeatedly invited and urged to repair to some of the neighbors, to spend the winter where he might be comfortable, absolutely declined, alleging that he had everything he wanted. He would not suffer any one to spend a night in his house, or to take care of him in his last illness. For several weeks before his death he was in a feeble state of health. . . .

"On Thursday night last week the cold was so extreme, that the mercury fell in Fahrenheit's thermometer to four degrees below 0. In the evening he was so well as to be laying out his business for the ensuing spring, but in the morning he was unable to rise. He had his senses, but soon expired. Almost anyone else would, in similar circumstances, have been totally frozen long before morning. According to his usual custom, he was without a shirt to his back, but was clad in an old, tattered cloth garb; and his only covering for the night, besides, was a small ragged blanket, and his bed was a parcel of straw."

Mr. Lear's mother, who lived in Portsmouth, became a centenarian, and it was felt that if her son had lived less sordidly and solitarily he too might have grown to be as old as the hills.

Samuel Nightingale, the hermit of Ashfield, Massachusetts, was refused burial in the cemetery because he was thought to be a wizard. He was one of the first settlers of the town and lived in a hut built against a rock.

In the pioneer period many men became temporary hermits, living alone for months in the wilderness while scouting for likely sites for new settlements or working at clearing the land in some chosen spot. But these men were not true hermits, any more than were the New England mariners who occasionally were shipwrecked on desert islands or lonely coasts, where they dragged out solitary existences until rescued. Hermitism with them was not a chosen career.

About the time of the Mexican War, the town of Westerly, Rhode Island, had an old and poor and timid hermit named Daniel Wilbur, who had neither house nor home. He was known as the Wild Man of Westerly, but was quite harmless and never bothered anyone. No reason is known for his becoming feral. The picture of him by the historian of Westerly is not unattractive.

"Seemingly gifted, but wholly uneducated, extremely eccentric, afraid of all human kind, even children, he was commonly called 'the wild man.' Having studied the stars, and the signs of the clouds and the winds, he was proverbially weatherwise, and was popularly named 'the astronomer.' In the summer he lived chiefly on berries and fruits, and slept in a swamp by the side of a large rock, having an old door as a kind of roof, and a bundle of flax for a pillow. In winter he fed on nuts, roots, such grain as he had stored, and such game as he could entrap. He would sometimes take refuge in a barn or shed, but rarely consented to enter a house. Though he traversed quite a region, he seldom allowed himself to be seen. In passing through the fields of farmers he displayed a singular penchant for scratching numbers, signs, and figures on the pumpkins."

Collectors of old stereoscope views prize highly the one showing English Jack, the Hermit of the White Mountains, standing outside his hermitage, a rough shack in the woods near the highway at the Gate of Crawford Notch. Hordes of summer tourists used to visit the House that Jack Built, many of them purchasing from the hermit souvenirs which he made during the winter when he could not get out to tend his line of traps.

One of the items he sold was a booklet containing the story of his life, in which he told how he had followed the seas for many years and had engaged in the search for Sir John Franklin, the Arctic explorer. He had suffered shipwreck, spending nineteen months on a desert island with four shipmates. He had fought in the Crimean War and served in India during the Mutiny. His life had been filled with adventure, but on returning to England he learned that his sweetheart had died. After that nothing mattered. He came to this country and, visiting the White Mountains, decided to settle there.

He became a professional hermit, successfully commercializing himself until his death in 1912 at the age of ninety. It used to be said of English Jack that he liked to eat snakes, but when questioned about this he said, "They ain't never ketched me at it."

It is an odd fact that while the climate of New England is hardly favorable to hermitism, many recluses have chosen some of the coldest and most exposed places in the region for their abodes. A favorite resort for them has been the islands of the Maine coast, where, though less well equipped than Robinson Crusoe was for his sequestration, they have nevertheless managed to exist, but under more or less haggard conditions, living mainly on gull soup and fish, perhaps supplemented by a few potatoes cultivated by the anchorites with a clam hoe.

In 1777 an Englishman named Thomas Kench, who had been with Arnold's expedition to Quebec, began a life of solitude in the Burnt Coat group of islands. He established himself on Harbor Island, which lies athwart the entrance to Burnt Coat Harbor at Swan's Island. He was anything but cordial when some other settlers on the coast spotted the smoke of his fire and in a spirit of neighborliness dropped in to see him. He said to them in effect, "Please go away." Kench lived alone among the islands for ten years. When Colonel James Swan bought the group from Massachusetts and began building a large house at Burnt Coat Harbor, the hermit withdrew.

Within the memory of living persons three hermits lived on Roque Island near Jonesport. They were brothers, but each kept to his own patch of woods and strip of beach. Boating parties from Jonesport used to circumnavigate the island in the hope of catching a glimpse of one of the eccentrics. All the brothers were bearded in traditional hermit style.

But sea hermits are not the only kind of which Maine can boast. Others have lived in the hinterland. Searsmont once had two of them. One was a man named Braddock, who arrived in pioneering times and became a forest dweller, choosing as his camp site a place near a pond. At his own request he was buried on an island in the pond.

The other was Timothy Barrett, a native of Concord, Massachusetts, who lived for thirty-five years near another pond, sleeping in a hollow log or cave. Civilization advancing too close to him, he retired up the west branch of George's River, locating at the head of a pond in Montville, where he died in 1847, at the reputed age of eighty-five.

There is a legend about a Maine hermit who lived on an island above the falls of the Androscoggin River at Lewiston. The Indians feared and misunderstood this isolationist and determined to murder him. So one dark night a party of fifty embarked in canoes well above the island and dropped silently downstream with the current, guided by what they took to be the light in the hermit's cabin. But the hermit, who had suspected their plans, had blacked out his cabin and by the use of a false light placed below his hermitage decoyed the murder party into the fast water above the falls. Before the Indians realized it they were caught and being swept helplessly along to their doom. The whole fleet went over the falls, and all hands were lost.

As a class the hermits of New England seem to have haunted the vicinity of ponds, or other bodies of water, fresh or salt. Perhaps this was on account of the fishing, but, whatever the cause, it was surely not because they liked to bathe.

Snake Hunters

THE old writers on the natural history of New England made up for the unreliability and sketchiness of what they had to say by the way in which they said it. Manner rather than matter was their long suit. Take the case of John Josselyn, for example, whose *New England's Rarities Discovered* was published in London in 1672 and was followed two years later by *An Account of Two Voyages to New England*. Any schoolboy could criticize many of the facts contained in these now rare volumes. Josselyn accepted, indeed, almost any kind of absurd legend. But his books, opened anywhere, reveal English prose of distinction and charm. In the form of his work is a spirit of beauty, substantial and alive, which must endure when works indubitably true as regards mere fact without that spirit must perish.

Of snakes he says, "There are infinite numbers of various colours, some black, others painted with red, yellow, and white, some again of a grass-green powdered all over as it were with silver dust or Muscovie-glass. But there is one that exceeds all the rest, and that is the Checkquered snake, having as many colours within the checkquers shadowing one another, as there are in a Rainbow."

Josselyn said he never heard of any mischief that snakes did, but they were sometimes killed for their skins to make hatbands of, and a skin worn as a garter was an excellent remedy against cramp. "The heart of a Rattle-snake dried and pulverized and drunk with wine or beer is an approved remedy against the biting and venome of a Rattle-snake," he declared.

Many towns in the southern half of New England had so many rattlesnakes that snake hunts were organized in the spring of the year to cut down their numbers or to annihilate them altogether. That many rattlers escaped these drives is shown by the fact that in some localities the species still exists.

As late as 1844, a bounty of a dollar a head was offered for rattlesnakes by Manchester, Massachusetts, and a man named John D. Hildreth won local renown for ridding the town of them. He made a business of catching them, not alone for the bounty, but for the oil, which was believed to have medicinal value and commanded a good price. He also disposed of live specimens to museums and showmen. In the milder months he hunted them with a dog to stir them up and a long stick with a slipnoose attached to the end to lasso them when they reared their heads to strike. In winter he caught them by building a fire at the mouths of their dens and when he had lured them forth flung them onto the snow, the chill of which took all the fight out of them. This stratagem worked so well that he succeeded in exterminating all the rattlesnakes in Manchester.

Another old-fashioned method used to kill reptiles was to catch one near his den, tie a powder horn with a lighted fuse to him, and then let him retreat into the den among the other snakes, where the horn exploded, like a grenade in a foxhole.

New England has had some mighty women snake killers. A hill in Canton, Connecticut, called Rattlesnake Mountain, commemorates the encounter between a large number of rattlesnakes and a Mrs. Wilcox, an early settler of the town, who met the snakes near the mountain while driving home her cows and slew forty of them, all full grown.

Massachusetts had a woman snake hunter who was noted for the number of rattlers she bagged. She lived on a farm in Sturbridge, near which was a noted haunt of these reptiles, where she used to go a-Maying for them. There is an interesting note about her in Barber.

"In the southern part of the township is an extensive tract of broken land, near which the Breakneck Pond in Union, Connecticut, takes its rise. A ledge of rock in this tract extends about a mile, which, in some places, is 100 feet perpendicular. This ledge has been a great place for rattlesnakes. It is stated that an old lady, the wife of an extensive farmer by the name of Howard, living in this vicinity, after her dairy business was done in the morning, in the month of May, used to go out and kill rattlesnakes; and that she had been known to kill as many as sixteen in one morning. These snakes, some years ago, were made considerable use of for medicinal purposes; the oil as a remedy for quinsy and sprains, the skin for rheumatism and headaches; and the gall was also used in medicinal preparations. They were worth from 50 to 75 cents per head, and it was for the profit of the business that it was followed by the old lady."

Various remedies were employed to counteract the ill effects of snake bites. Warm milk baths, the application of fresh earth, or the skins of freshly killed sheep were among the remedies used. Ebenezer Tappan of Manchester, Massachusetts, who survived the bite of a rattler, felt the effects of the venom until his death forty years later. Every year, about the time when he had been bitten, his skin where the snake had struck him was said to become inflamed and discolored, and he experienced the discomfort of lameness.

The Indian cure for snake bites was snakeroot. On Indiantown Island, in the backwaters of the Sheepscot River, near Boothbay Harbor, Maine, is the traditional site of an Indian herb garden, a sandy plain some two or three acres in extent, lying between the elevated central part of the island and the rocky bluff on the western side, where, it is said, strange plants of medicinal virtue were grown by the Indians, and where snakeroot still thrives, though Maine has no poisonous snakes.

Next to the rattler and the copperhead, the black snake, though a nonvenomous constrictor, was probably the most feared of New England snakes. Formerly one heard much more about them, particularly of their great size, some of them being upward of nine feet long, and of their attacks on people. Cases were even reported of black snakes dropping on their intended victims from the branches of trees. One case, I recall, was that of a girl who was attacked while playing croquet.

Preserved in the annals of the town of Yarmouth on Cape Cod is an anecdote of Joseph Nauhaught, an Indian deacon, who once stirred up a den of these black reptiles and was almost overwhelmed by them. Although the modern reader may find the incident improbable, Nauhaught was not, as some may think, a drinking Indian, but a praying one, a pious and worthy character, whose adventure with the snakes is said to be well authenticated.

"Deacon Nauhaught was once attacked by a number of large black snakes. Being at a distance from any inhabitants, he was, to be sure, in a very precarious situation; for, unfortunately, he had not even a knife about him for his defence. To outrun them, he found utterly impossible; to keep them off without any weapon was equally so. He therefore came to the determination to stand firm on his feet. They began winding themselves about him; in a little time, one of them had made his way up to the Indian's neck, and was trying to put his black head into his mouth. Nauhaught opened it immediately. *The black serpent thrust in his head, and Nauhaught, putting his jaws together, bit it off in a moment!* As soon as the blood, streaming from the beheaded, was discovered by the snakes, they left their intended prey with great precipitation, and Nauhaught was liberated from the jaws of impending death."

There used to be a New England superstition that anyone who would catch a blacksnake and bite through it to the backbone would have good teeth all his life.

Probably the most wonderful snake ever to appear in New England was the double-headed snake of Newbury, which had a head at each end of its body. Whittier wrote a poem about this remarkable reptile, basing it upon a letter from the Reverend Christopher Tappan to Cotton Mather. The letter, which as evidence is nothing but hearsay, reads in part as follows:

"Concerning the Amphisbeana," writes Mr. Tappan,

"as soon as I received your commands I made diligent enquiry of several persons who saw it after it was dead. . . . They directed me, for further information, . . . to the persons who saw it alive, and killed it, which were two or three lads, about twelve or fourteen; one of which, a pert, sensible youngster, told me that one of his mates, running towards him, cryed out there was a snake with two heads running after him, upon which he run to him; and the snake getting into a puddle of water, he with a stick pulled him out, after which it came towards him, and as he went backwards and forward, so the snake would do likewise. After a little time, the snake, upon his striking at him, gathered up his whole body into a sort of quoil, except *both heads,* which kept towards him, and he distinctly saw two *mouths* and two *stings* (as they are vulgarly called), which stings or tongues it kept putting forth after the usual manner of snakes till he killed it. . . .

"*Postscript.*—Before ensealing I spoke with the other man who examined the Amphisbeana (and he is also a man of credit), and he assured me that it had really two heads, one at each end, two mouths, two stings, or tongues, and so forth.

"Sir, I have nothing more to add, but that he may have a remembrance in your prayers who is,

"Sir, your most humble servant,
"Christopher Tappan."

Whittier composed *The Double-Headed Snake of Newbury* in 1859. Part of the poem reads as follows:

Far and wide the tale was told,
Like a snowball growing while it rolled.

The nurse hushed with it the baby's cry:
And it served in the worthy minister's eye,
To paint the primitive serpent by.
Cotton Mather came galloping down
All the way to Newbury town,
With his eyes agog and his ears set wide,
And his marvellous inkhorn at his side;
Stirring the while in the shallow pool
Of his brains for the lore he learned at school,
To garnish the story, with here a streak
Of Latin, and there another of Greek:
And the tales he heard and the notes he took,
Behold! are they not in his Wonder-Book?

Among the tall tales of the late Louis T. (Lou) Stone of Winsted, Connecticut, whose fantastic nature anecdotes went round the world, were a number of snake stories, one of which was revived recently when it was made the subject of a mural in the Winchester Hotel, Winsted, where there is a series of paintings illustrating some of the most famous of Lou Stone's stories. The anecdote, which goes back to the early days of the automobile, is about a rattlesnake that bit an automobile tire. Air escaping from the puncture blew up the snake till it burst. A somewhat similar story, concerning a snake that swallowed a stick of dynamite purchased by a man to blow up stumps in his garden, was printed in Lou Stone's paper, the *Winsted-Citizen,* at the beginning of the century, and may be taken as a typical example of his special brand of Yankee humor.

"Snakes seem to be plenty in the neighborhood of Goshen, if stories wafted down from that region are correct. Dynamite is a sweetish sort of stuff and snakes love sweet stuff. A big, black snake about seven feet long was in a man's garden near the forest, and crawled under the hog pen just as the man picked up a rock and threw it at the reptile. The rock hit the snake, however, which probably having swallowed one of the sticks of dynamite, exploded and blew himself into smithereens, demolishing also the corner of the hog pen, which now gives silent testimony of the truth of the story. The hog was scared half to death, but was not otherwise hurt, as he was in the front of the pen. The man who owned the hog and the stick of dynamite was also badly scared, but was not hurt. The man's name is Igney Androsky, a Pole or Prussian, who vouches for the story, but says in extenuation of the act of blowing up a snake by striking him with a stone, that he 'didn't know dot snake vas loaded.' "

Josselyn said that the chief or captain of snakes was the rattler, but he forgot the sea serpent, which he was himself the first to report on the seacoast of New England. When Josselyn joined his brother at Black Point, Scarborough, Maine, in 1638, some of the neighbors came to welcome him to this country, and the tales they told the newcomer were very tall ones indeed.

"One Mr. *Mitten*," for example, "related of a *Triton* or *Mereman* which he saw in *Cascobay,* the Gentleman was a great Fowler, and used to go out with a small Boat or Canow, and fetching a compass about a small Island, (there being many small Islands in the Bay) for the advantage of a shot, was encountered with a *Triton,* who laying his hands upon the side of the Canow, had one of them chopt off with a Hatchet by Mr. *Mitten,* which was in all respects like the hand of a man, the *Triton* presently sunk, dyeing the water with his purple blood and was no more seen."

They also told him "of a young Lyon [not long be-
fore] kill'd at *Piscataway* by an *Indian,* of a *Sea-Serpent*
or *Snake,* that lay quoiled up like a Cable upon a Rock at
Cape-Ann: a Boat passing by with English aboard, and
two *Indians,* they would have shot the *Serpent,* but the
Indians disswaded them, saying, that if he were not kill'd
outright, they would all be in danger of their lives."

Since this first report the sea serpent has appeared repeatedly on the New England coast. It is true that of late
years it has proved shy and its appearances have been
rare, but not so many years ago it could be counted on to
show itself several times a summer, and there was not
a seaside hotel proprietor or breezy old salt along the
seaboard who could not vouch for having seen it at one
time or another. And always their reports were made
with the greatest circumstantiality and conviction. The
direction and rate of speed of the serpent were always
noted with particularity, and it was, of course, invariably
of prodigious size and possessed all the characteristics as-
cribed to it by the ancient writers, even to swimming with
a wavy up-and-down movement, instead of the undulating
sideways motion of ordinary serpents. One year there
were so many reports of the serpent in the vicinity of
Nahant near Boston that some of Massachusetts' best
whalemen were engaged in hunting it, but none got within
striking distance.

Preachers and
Deacons

IT IS a mistake to suppose that in the early days New England was a gloomy land. Despite the austerity of its creed and the rigor of its laws, cheerfulness was always breaking in, though life under frontier conditions had its hardships and limitations and other times had other ways. The Puritans were a devout people who took their religion seriously, but religion and humor are not incompatible. Many New England ministers were extremely witty men, who, when anything amusing happened at meeting, had difficulty in maintaining a poker face in the pulpit. Some deliberately indulged their senses of humor in addressing their congregations.

When Dr. Mather Byles of Boston had to deliver a sermon because the Reverend Mr. Prince, who was expected to preach, failed to appear, he took for his text, "Put not your trust in princes." On the famous Dark Day of May 19, 1780, when a remarkable dimness settled over New England and many people thought the day of judgment was at hand, a woman sent her young son to Dr. Byles to know if he could tell her the cause of the obscurity.

"My dear, give my compliments to your mother," he said to the messenger, "and tell her I am as much in the dark as she is."

A clergyman who preached one Sunday morning in the rocky town of Pelham, Massachusetts, begged for funds for the college in the adjoining town of Amherst. The contribution boxes were passed, but the Scotch Presbyterians of Pelham, perhaps because they had already contributed supplies of building material to the college, wouldn't give a cent. When the visiting parson saw the boxes returned empty, a smile flickered half apologetically across his face as he gave out for the closing hymn the one by Watts with the opening lines,

> Lord, what a wretched land is this,
> That yields us no supplies!

Even an occasion as solemn as the consecration of a new meeting house had its lighter side. When the Old Tunnel Meeting House at Lynn, Massachusetts, was dedicated in 1682, a noble and savory banquet of fat things was served such as was never before known in the history of the town.

"Ye Deddication Dinner was had in ye greate barne of Mr. Hoode," reads a contemporary account of the affair, "which by reason of its goodly size was deemed ye most fit place. It was neatly adorned with green bows and other hangings and made very faire to look upon, ye wreaths being mostly wrought by ye young folk, they meeting together, both maides and young men, and having a merry time in doing ye work. Ye rough stalls and unhewed posts being gaily begirt and all ye corners and cubbies being

clean swept and well aired, it truly did appear a meet ban-
quetting hall. Ye scaffolds too from which ye provinder
had been removed were swept cleane as broome could
make them. Some seats were put up on ye scaffolds where-

on might sitt such of ye antient women as would see &
ye maides and children. Ye greate floor was all held for ye
company which was to partake of ye feast of fat things,
none others being admitted there save them that were to
wait upon ye same. Ye kine that were wont to be there
were forced to keep holiday in the field."

The farm fowls proved an abominable nuisance, constantly flying into the barn and perching above the table at which the visiting clergy sat. Not satisfied with merely a bird's-eye view of the festivities, they scattered feathers, hay, and fine particles on the diners below. The Reverend Jeremiah Shepard, the minister of the new meeting house, who suffered most outrageously from the attentions of the birds, jumped up from his seat, his face very red, and, grabbing an apple from the table, let drive at the feathered offenders on the rafters. But this only made matters worse. It created a terrible rumpus among the fowls, and a large rooster, who was knocked off his perch by the well-aimed fruit, came flopping and floundering down on the table, spilling drinks and scattering gravy, sauce, and other things on the garments and in the faces of the banqueters.

This mishap, however, was greeted with general merriment, in which the ministers joined, though the laughter of some was perhaps a little forced, while a few were definitely not amused. But as the fowls persisted in their invasion and the roosters to crow derisively, the most dignified parsons at length joined in the sport of repelling them with apples and nuts.

"Dainty meats were on ye table in great plenty," the account continues, "bear-stake, deer-meat, rabbit, and fowls, both wild and from ye barnyard. Luscious puddings we likewise had in abundance, mostly apple and berry, but some of corn meal with small bits of sewet baked therein; also pyes and tarts. We had some pleasant fruits, as apples, nuts and wild grapes, and to crown all, we had plenty of good cider and ye inspiring Barbadoes drink."

Some of the older ministers solemnly discussed the points of the dedication sermon, or the comeliness of the new house of worship, or with perhaps even greater relish

labored silently at their food. But some of the younger
parsons were out to make a jolly time of it. The Reverend Joseph Gerrish of Wenham seems to have been the
life of the party, keeping those at his end of the table in
a continuous state of merriment. There were outbreaks
of loud laughter and bursts of hand-clapping.

Once he grievously scandalized Mr. Shepard, "who suddenly looking up from his dish did spy him, as he thot,
winking in an unbecoming way at one of ye pretty damsels
on ye scaffold." Bidding the godly Mr. Rogers to labor
with him aside for his misbehavings, it turned out that the
winking was occasioned by some of the hayseed that was
blowing about lodging in his eye. Mr. Shepard was greatly
relieved.

Although prudent in his meat and drink, Mr. Gerrish
continued in jovial mood, until at the height of the rejoic-
ings a strange disaster befell him. "Not having his thots
about him he endeavored ye dangerous performance of
gaping and laughing at the same time which he must now
feel is not so easy or safe a thing. In doing this he set his
jaws open in such wise that it was beyond all his power to
bring them together again. His agonie was very great, and
his joyful laugh soon turned to grievous groaning. Ye
women in ye scaffold became much distressed for him. We
did our utmost to stay ye anguish of Mr. Gerrish, but
could make out little till Mr. Rogers who knoweth somewhat of anatomy did bid ye sufferer to sit down on ye floor,
which being done Mr. Rogers took ye head atween his
legs, turning ye face upward as much as possible and then
gave a powerful blow and then sudden press which brot
ye jaws into working order. But Mr. Gerrish did not gape
or laugh much more on that occasion, neither did he talk
much for that matter."

There were a few "mawdlin songs and much roistering laughter," very mortifying to some of those present, but no other serious mishaps occurred, "Save that one of ye Salem delegates, in boastfully essaying to crack a walnut atween his teeth did crack, instead of ye nut, a most usefull double tooth and was thereby forced to appear at ye evening with bandaged face."

Thus, with the help of a sermon, savory meats, and plenty of old Barbadoes, was the meeting house at Lynn dedicated in the Pilgrim century.

Everybody drank without prejudice in those days, including the clergy, some of whom displayed a remarkable capacity for intoxicants. People drank on all occasions and on the slightest pretext. They did it at weddings, funerals, elections, ordinations, house raisings, and auctions. An auctioneer would flourish a bottle before a crowd, offering a drink to the next person who would raise the bid. Someone would raise it a cent and get the drink and be the envy of all. People liked hard cider and sound doctrine. Hard cider made ugly drunks, and cider brandy or applejack, which is made by distilling cider, is said to have been the cause of the death of more mothers-in-law in New England than any other. A tough old swamp Yankee after he had drunk liberally of applejack was apt to reach for the family musket and cry, "Whar is she?"

It was rumored that the Reverend Robert Abercrombie from Scotland, who was pastor of the Presbyterian church at Pelham in the eighteenth century, was wont to get a wee bit fou' more often than was good for him. The charge, winning plausibility through repetition, was so persistently circulated that at length the members of the church felt that they could no longer ignore it. Accordingly, a meeting was called to consider the matter, at which a committee of three was chosen to call on the pastor and in a temperate spirit inform him of the charge and if there was found to be any truth in it to remonstrate with him about his conduct. The committee was to report to the church body at the next regular meeting.

Learning about the meeting, Mr. Abercrombie instructed his wife to observe the customary etiquette in the case of visitors by mixing drinks for the committee. The first round was to be well-watered rum. The second round was to contain less water and more rum, while the third was to consist of nothing but rum. The committee came in the evening and was greeted cordially by the pastor, who, when they told him their errand, took it in good part, saying he was sorry if he had given any cause for complaint. He said he appreciated the kindly way in which the committee had done its duty and he hoped the same spirit of kindliness and charity would mark their report to the church.

With the official and embarrassing part of their call over, the members settled down to enjoy a pleasant social evening with their pastor. Round followed round of drinks until at last the Abercrombie parlor looked like an alcoholic ward, with the three committeemen stretched out on the floor completely overcome by the rum. Two of them didn't get home until morning, the third not until noon. Everybody wondered what they would say in their report to the church. They reported that they had called on Mr. Abercrombie and he had given them satisfaction.

Then there is the story of the parson at Ashfield, Massachusetts, who mounted his horse one afternoon to make parish calls. He was, of course, offered a glass of toddy at each house he visited, and by the time he came to make his last call was unmistakably feeling the effects of the drinks he had taken. But he dismounted at the last house, drew the bridle rein over his horse's head, and threw it over the hitching post. While he was inside making his call, during which he had another drink, his horse got loose, but was promptly caught by a neighbor who secured the animal to the post again by passing the rein through the augur hole near the top and then looping it over the post. When the minister finished his call and came out to go home he had difficulty unhitching his horse. Finally, after he had delayed some time, members of the family who had been watching came to his assistance. Glassy-eyed but dignified, the D.D. explained the situation.

"Friends," he said, "since I have been in your house one of the most remarkable miracles ever known has occurred, for my horse has in some manner crawled through the hole in this post, and I cannot persuade him to return."

The first book on the subject of humor published in America was printed at Boston in 1707. It was called *The Government and Improvement of Mirth According to the Laws of Christianity*. It was written by Benjamin Colman, who said his little work was especially designed for the use of young people, and he recommended it particularly to the serious perusal of the young men of Boston. The book consists of three sermons, in the first of which Mr. Colman deals with civil and natural mirth, in the second with carnal and vicious humor, and in the third with spiritual and holy joy. There is scarcely a phase of the subject that he does not explore. Admitting that there is express scriptural allowance for mirth and that laughter may be highly ornamental to the Christian life, as well as of great use to refresh and recruit tired nature in her work, he insists that it must be moderate.

"The measure of mirth may be prodigal and intemperate," he says. "There is a mean to be kept in all things. No excess is innocent. Mirth may be immoderate in the degree of it. Excessive *loud* it sometimes is, and sometimes excessive *long*. The first is too often to be heard in taverns, when drink has intoxicated men and banish'd reason and sobriety. They chant to the sound of the viol, but their own voice is most criminal. Inferior mariners especially give themselves this offensive license. A gag is their proper and due punishment."

But on the whole Mr. Colman's little treatise is reasonable and human.

Eccentric ministers were no rarity in New England. One preacher adhered to the unusual practice of wearing a black handkerchief over his face. This was the Reverend Joseph Moody of York, Maine, who was ordained the first minister of the second parish in 1732. Because he appeared with his face covered, he was called Handkerchief Moody. Hawthorne wrote a dismal story about the circumstance of the handkerchief, and in a note to the tale said the reason for it was that in early life Handkerchief had accidentally killed a beloved friend. Tradition, however, seems to be the only authority that supports this statement. Handkerchief Moody fell into a settled state of melancholy when his wife died, and it was then that he took to hiding his features. He must have caused a sensation the first Sunday he climbed into the pulpit masked like a bandit. One wonders if it muffled his preaching and made him sound as if he were talking through a blanket.

For over a century ministers wore wigs. The last of the Connecticut clergy to give up the wig was the Reverend John Marsh, D.D., of Wethersfield, who died in 1820

at the age of seventy-nine. "I have often seen him in it,"
says Samuel G. Goodrich, "though he left it off a short
time before his death. . . . For many years he was accustomed to mount his old chaise and set off with Mrs.
Marsh to attend the annual commencement at Cambridge
College. Everybody knew him along the road, and bowing
as he passed, said 'How d'ye do, Dr. Marsh?' At last he
dismissed his wig; but now, as he went along, nobody recognized him. It was evident that his wig was necessary to
insure the accustomed and grateful salute; so, on his
journeys to commencement ever after, he put it on, though
he discarded it at other times."

Another story told of Dr. Marsh concerns his attending
commencement at Yale College. A gentleman from Virginia who chanced to be in New Haven on the jubilee day
decided to see the ceremonies. He followed the crowd to
the chapel where he asked to be admitted. It was the custom then to receive the reverend clergy and ladies first,
and, after they had been accommodated in seats especially
reserved for them, to admit the general public. The door-
keeper looked over the Virginian as he approached and,
seeing him to be a distinguished gentleman of fifty in black,
with a trace of powder on his collar, took him to be a
minister of the Gospel and let him pass. Inside, the sexton
ushered him to a seat among the D.D.'s, placing him in a
pew next to old Dr. Marsh.

The southerner sat down and looked about the chapel.
New Haven was then celebrated for the beauty of its
women. The gentleman's gaze soon fell upon a battery
of eyes, beautiful yet dangerous, peeping down from the
gallery. "Unconscious of the sanctity and saintliness of his
position, he half rose and made a low and gracious bow to
the ladies above, as if to challenge their whole artillery.

Every eye in the house was thus drawn toward him. Before he had time to compose himself, Miss F——, one of the belles of the day, came down the broad aisle, full upon him! He had never seen anything so marvelously beautiful—at once so simple and so superb, so much a woman and so much a divinity. He held his breath until she had passed, when he turned suddenly to Rev. Dr. Marsh, and giving him a slap on his shoulder—which dislodged a shower of powder from his wig—exclaimed, 'By all the gods, sir, there is Venus herself.' "

Some of the most eccentric preachers were the illiterate propagandists of the early days of Methodism, when the doctrine was held that learning was a handicap rather than a help to a preacher and spiritual gifts and grace were what counted—a view also held by the early Baptists. Many of these unlettered men, like the famous Lorenzo Dow, were effective speakers who scored heavily with the backwoods people to whom they spoke. Their rough and ready way of preaching was more appreciated by the audiences they addressed than the cultivated, academic style of sermonizing. One of these shabby characters, during a discourse delivered somewhere in Connecticut, is reported to have spoken as follows:

"What I insist upon, my brethren and sisters, is this: larnin isn't religion, and eddication don't give a man the power of the Spirit. It is grace and gifts that furnish the real live coals from off the altar. St. Peter was a fisherman—do you think he ever went to Yale College? Yet he was the rock upon which Christ built his Church. No, no, beloved brethren and sisters. When the Lord wanted to blow down the walls of Jericho, he didn't take a brass trumpet, or a polished French horn: no such thing; he took a ram's horn—a plain, natural ram's horn—just as it grew. And so, when he wants to blow down the walls of the spiritual Jericho, my beloved brethren and sisters, he don't take one of your smooth, polite, college larnt gentlemen, but a plain, natural ram's-horn sort of a man like me."

New England used to be plagued by bogus ministers who circulated through the region bent on all kinds of buzzardry. Among the better class of old-time rogues, particularly those who were possessed of a little learning and were not too evil of countenance, masquerading as a parson seems to have been one of the stock items in the strolling man's bag of tricks. At one time there was confined in Newgate prison in Connecticut a convict who was famous for his success in passing himself off as a cleric. He was a glib humbug, and on the expiration of his sentence, one of his fellow convicts, seeing him pass out of the prison gate, cried, "Woe to the inhabitants of the earth, for the devil has gone among them!"

Another part which this rascal is said to have played to perfection was impersonating a missing person. When he heard of the absence of a long-lost friend or relative of a family, he would appear and say he was that person. In one case he claimed to be the stray husband of a disconsolate woman, and so cleverly did he play the part that she welcomed him with open arms. Only when he was taking off his shoes did she suspect him. She remarked that he had more toes than her husband, who had lost one by amputation. But the rogue had a ready explanation. He said, "It growed out again."

The fraudulent parson did not as a rule attempt to fool a whole community for a considerable period of time, as did the notorious Stephen Burroughs the town of Pelham, but rather to victimize a single person quickly, and then get away as speedily as possible. A typical case, in

which a sham parson rehabilitated himself at the expense
of a genuine one, was reported in the *American Mercury*
of May 2, 1785. The victim, incidentally, was the minister
with whom Stephen Burroughs lived for a while when pre-
paring for college.

"By authentic information from Connecticut, we learn
that a few weeks since, a person on his travels through
the town of Coventry in that state, stopped on a Satur-
day at the house of the Rev. Joseph Huntington, D.D.
and acquainted the Doctor that he had been preaching at
Susquehannah for a considerable time, was so unfortunate
as to be driven from his possessions there by the Indians—that his property was destroyed by them—that he
was then bound to the state of Massachusetts, where he
had some friends residing, and at the same time begged
charity. The Doctor, who is by no means a stranger to
the acts of hospitality, was very liberal and charitable to
the clergyman, and invited him to stay and spend the Sabbath, as there would be an impropriety in his traveling the
following day; which invitation the stranger accepted. The
Doctor then requested his brother clergyman to assist him
in the duties of his function; but he objected, and said his
clothes were not sufficiently decent to appear in the pulpit.

"In order to obviate this difficulty, the Doctor offered
him a suit of clothes which he had not long since received
from the tailor, and desired him to try them on, which he
did, and found they suited very well. The objection being
removed, the clergyman accordingly agreed to assist the
Doctor the succeeding day, and desired to be by himself
that evening to study his discourse. A fire was then made
in his bed chamber, where he repaired with his new garb,
at the same time acquainting the Doctor that he must study

until late at night, and hoped that no noise he might make would disturb the repose of the family.

"Sunday morning came, the adroit clergyman was sent for to breakfast, but to the great surprise of the family, he was not to be found; for during the night he had taken his exit, not forgetting the garments so well suited to his clerical dignity, and leaving behind him the following select and well adapted text, prefixed at the top of the paper intended for his sermon. 'Ye shall seek me and shall not find me; and where I am, thither ye cannot come.' —John 7, 34."

The deacons of the old-time New England churches were the grave and reverend seniors of their communities. Adhering to the highest standards in the conduct of their lives, they set an example and were respected and esteemed by all. To address any man as deacon was to confer an honorary title of the first order. In the meeting house the deacons used to sit together, sometimes in high-backed chairs, in a special pew that was elevated above the rest, and by all accounts they formed an awe-inspiring group.

There is an old New England saying, "All deacons are good, but there's odds in deacons," meaning that among these pillars of the church one finds eccentrics. One such deacon was Captain Reynol Marvin of Lyme, Connecticut, whose life was governed almost entirely by communications which he believed came directly from the Lord. His courtship was typical of the way he did things. One day he mounted his horse with only a sheepskin for a saddle and rode to the home of Betty Lee. Without dismounting, he requested Betty to come to him. On her coming out of the house, he said that the Lord had sent him there to marry her. And without much hesitation, Betty said, "The Lord's will be done."

Another time he announced that the Lord had directed him to distribute his cows among his poor neighbors. This he proceeded to do, but when the distribution had been going on for some time, a man who feared he was not going to get one went to the deacon and told him he had received a communication from the Lord, saying that the Lord had directed him to the deacon for a cow.

"Well," said Deacon Marvin, "you shall receive it. What cow did the Lord say should be given you, a new milch or a farrow?"

"A milch cow," said the man.

"Well," replied the deacon, "your communication could not have been from the Lord, for I have already given away all my new milch cows."

There were a few deacons who were given to hypocritical posing and to practices inconsistent with their position in the church, and these Christian cads lowered the general esteem in which the deaconry was held. "I don't know how it is," wrote Samuel G. Goodrich in 1856, "but the term *deacon* is associated in many minds with a certain littleness, and especially of a sort of affectation and cant in conversation, an I-am-holier-than-thou air and manner."

He cited the case of the Hartford deacon who was in the crockery and furniture business with his son Laertes. This deacon deemed it proper to be very scriptural in his speech and to talk as much as possible like Isaiah. One day, when a female customer entered the store, the deacon, who was engaged with another customer, went to call his son who was busy in the loft above. Placing himself at the foot of the stairs and attuning his voice to the occasion, he said, "La-ar-tes descend—a lady waits!"

This same deacon also tried to signalize himself by a special attitude toward the ways of Providence, and would never take out any fire insurance, saying that if the Lord wished to burn down his house or barn he would submit without a murmur. He pretended to consider thunder and lightning and conflagrations as special acts of the Almighty, and any attempt to avert their effects was distrusting Providence. In spite of the deacon's philosophy, Hartford managed to become one of the great insurance centers of the country.

A practical joke played on a deacon one Sunday morning in church so amused the minister that it was several minutes before he could continue preaching. Looking up in the midst of his sermon, he noticed one of his deacons fast asleep, his head resting against the back rail of the pew, his mouth wide open. Then he saw a young man in the gallery directly above the sleeping elder remove a quid of tobacco from his mouth and, taking careful aim, drop it, plop, into the deacon's open mouth. Thus sud-denly awakened from his nap, the deacon, scared half out of his senses, sat up choking and spluttering and continued to cough and fume for some time before he recovered. It is safe to say that if the deacon slept in meeting again, it was well out in the center of the church, and not in the lee of either the port or starboard gallery.

Everybody has heard of the old-fashioned horsy deacon who could not resist the temptation of doing a little horse trading on the Sabbath. He was a traditional Yankee type. Henry Ward Beecher has told of a fishing deacon who, on his way to meeting with his wife, used to drive past a mill pond in which there was a huge trout, a veritable Moby Dick of a fish, which everyone for miles around had tried and failed to catch. Always as the dea-

con drove by the pond on Sunday morning he would see
the trout leap, which sorely tempted him to play hookey
and try his hand at catching the big fish. He thought the
trout knew Sunday as well as he did and tried to annoy
him. The deacon loved to tell the story, and here it is in
the deacon's words as reported by Henry Ward Beecher
in his book of New England village life.

"One Sunday morning, just as I got along by the willows, I heard an awful splash, and not ten feet from the
shore I saw the trout, as long as my arm, just curving
over like a bow, and going down with something for breakfast. 'Gracious!' says I, and I almost jumped out of the
wagon. But my wife Polly, says she, 'What on airth are
you thinkin' of, Deacon? It's Sabbath-day, and you're
goin' to meetin'! It's pretty business for a deacon!' That
sort of talk cooled me off. But I do say, that for about a
minute I wished I wasn't a deacon. But 'twouldn't make
any difference, for I came down next day to mill on purpose, and I came down once or twice more, and nothin'
was to be seen, tho' I tried him with the most temptin'
things. Wall, next Sunday I came along agin, and to save
my life I couldn't keep off worldly and wandering
thoughts. I tried to be sayin' my Catechism. But I couldn't
keep my eyes off the pond as we came to the willows. I'd
got along in the Catechism as smooth as the road, to the
Fourth Commandment, and was sayin' out loud for Polly,
and just as I was sayin': 'What is required in the Fourth
Commandment?' I heard a splash, and there was the trout,
and afore I could think, I said, 'Gracious, Polly; I must
have that trout.' She almost riz right up: 'I knew you
wasn't sayin' your Catechism hearty. Is this the way you
answer the question about keepin' the Lord's day? I'm
ashamed, Deacon Marble,' says she. 'You'd better change

your road, and go to meetin' on the road over the hill. If I was a deacon, I wouldn't let a fish's tail whisk the whole Catechism out of my head'; and I had to go to meetin' on the hill road all the rest of the summer."

To describe deacons and other laymen who are active in church affairs as pillars of the church is to use an old New England expression that originated in New Haven Colony in 1639. This colony, under the leadership of the Reverend John Davenport, was organized in accordance with the laws of the Bible. Only members of the church were allowed to vote and hold office, and the colonists agreed that the Bible had all the answers to every problem of church and state. On June 4, 1639, Mr. Davenport preached a sermon from Proverbs: "Wisdom hath builded her home; she hath hewn out her seven pillars." Following the sermon seven lay officers were chosen called Pillars of the Church.

Campus Character

MANY Yankee types of bygone days, from the Bare-foot Boy to the Village Blacksmith, are familiar to us through the work of the New England poets. Older than any of these, but now almost forgotten, is the character about whom John Seccomb wrote some humorous verses which delighted New Englanders for more than a century.

In 1730, there died at Cambridge, Massachusetts, a man named Matthew Adby, who for many years was a bedmaker and sweeper at Harvard College, a campus character if there ever was one. John Seccomb, who was graduated from Harvard in 1728, was still living and studying in Cambridge when the old bedmaker died. Seccomb had amused his friends with his undergraduate verse and could not resist taking the opportunity offered by Adby's death to compose a humorous poem listing the personal possessions which Adby might have left to his widow, Ruth, who, like himself, was a bedmaker and

sweeper at the college. Seccomb called his poem, which
was written in December, 1730, "Father Abbey's Will,"
and followed it in January, 1731, with "A Letter of
Courtship to his Amiable and Virtuous Widow," which
is supposed to be written by a bedmaker and sweeper at
Yale College. On the publication of the two poems, which
were printed together at Boston in 1731, Governor Jonathan Belcher sent copies to London, where they were re-
printed in the *London Magazine* and the *Gentlemen's
Magazine*. Here are these poems of yesteryear.

FATHER ABBEY'S WILL

Cambridge, December 30, 1730.

"Some time since died here, Mr. Matthew Abbey in a
very advanced age: He had for a great many years served
the College in quality of Bedmaker and Sweeper: Having
no child, his wife inherits his whole estate which he be-
queathed to her by his last will and testament, as follows,
viz.

> To my dear wife,
> My joy and life,
> I freely now do give her,
> My whole estate,
> With all my plate,
> Being just about to leave her.
>
> My tub of soap,
> A long cart-rope,
> A fryingpan and kettle,
> An ashes' pail,
> A thrashing-flail,
> An iron wedge and beetle.

Two painted chairs,
Nine warden pears,
A large old dripping platter,
This bed of hay,
On which I lay,
An old saucepan for batter.

A little mug,
A ten-quart jug,
A bottle full of brandy,
A looking-glass,
To see your face,
You'll find it very handy.

A musket true,
As ever flew,
A pound of shot and wallet,
A leather sash,
My calabash,
My powder-horn and bullet.

An old sword-blade,
A garden spade,
A hoe, a rake, a ladder,
A wooden can,
A close-stool pan,
A clyster pipe and bladder.

A greasy hat,
My old ram cat,
A yard and half of linen,
A woollen fleece,
A pot of grease,
In order for your spinning.

A small-tooth comb,
An ashen broom,
A candlestick and hatchet,
A coverlid,
Strip'd down with red,
A bag of rags to patch it.

Harvard University, Cambridge

A ragged mat,
A tub of fat,
A book put out by Bunyan,
Another book,
By Robin Cook,
A skein or two of spun yarn.

An old black muff,
Some garden-stuff,
A quantity of borage,
Some devil's weed,
And burdock seed,
To season well your porridge.

A chafing-dish,
With one salt-fish
If I am not mistaken,
A leg of pork,
A broken fork,
And half a flitch of bacon.

A spinning-wheel,
One peck of meal,
A knife without a handle,
A rusty lamp,
Two quarts of samp,
And half a tallow-candle.

My pouch and pipes,
Two oxen tripes,
An oaken dish well carved,
My little dog,
And spotted hog,
With two young pigs just starved.

This is my store,
I have no more,
I heartily do give it.
My years are spun,
My days are done,
And so I think to leave it.

Thus Father Abbey left his spouse,
As rich as church or college mouse,
Which is sufficient invitation,
To serve the college in his station."

A LETTER OF COURTSHIP TO HIS AMIABLE
AND VIRTUOUS WIDOW

Newhaven, January 2, 1731.

"Our sweeper having lately buried his spouse, and accidentally hearing of the death and will of his deceased Cambridge brother, has conceived a violent passion for the relict. As love softens the mind and disposes to poetry, he has eas'd himself in the following strains, which he transmits to the charming widow, as the first essay of his love and courtship.

> Mistress Abbey
> To you I fly,
> You only can relieve me.
> To you I turn,
> For you I burn,
> If you will but believe me.
>
> Then, gentle dame,
> Admit my flame,
> And grant me my petition,
> If you deny,
> Alas! I die
> In pitiful condition.
>
> Before the news
> Of your dead spouse
> Had reached us at Newhaven,
> My dear wife dy'd,
> Who was my bride
> In anno eighty-seven.
>
> Thus being free
> Let's both agree

To join our hands, for I do
   Boldly aver
   A widower
Is fittest for a widow.

   You may be sure
   'Tis not your dow'r
I make this flaming verse on;
   In these smooth lays
   I only praise
The glories of your person.

   For the whole that
   Was left by *Mat*
Fortune to me has granted
   In equal store,
   I've only one thing more
Which Matthew long had wanted.

   No teeth 'tis true
   You have to shew,
The young think teeth inviting;
   But, silly youths!
   I love those mouths
Where there's no fear of biting.

   A leaky eye
   That's never dry,
These woeful times is fitting.
   A wrinkled face
   Adds solemn grace
To folks devout at meeting.

A furrowed brow,
Where corn might grow,
Such fertile soil is seen in't,
A long hooked nose,
Tho' scorned by foes,
For spectacles convenient.

Thus to go on
I would put down
Your charms from head to foot,
Set all your glory
In verse before ye,
But I've no mind to do't.

Then haste away,
And make no stay;
For soon as you come hither,
We'll eat and sleep,
Make beds and sweep
And talk and smoke together.

But if, my dear,
I must move there,
Tow'ds Cambridge straight I'll see me,
To touse the hay
On which you lay,
If age and you will let me."

The widow never remarried, but continued to serve the college long after her husband's death. In the Boston *Evening Post* of Monday, December 13, 1762, the following notice concerning her appeared.

"Cambridge, Dec. 10. Yesterday died here in a very

advanced age [93] Mrs. Adby, Sweeper for many years at Harvard College, and well known to all that have had an education within the present Century. She was relict of Matthew Adby, Sweeper, well known to the learned world by his last Will and Testament."

John Seccomb, who was born in Medford in 1708, became a Congregational minister. He was for a number of years minister of the church at Harvard, Massachusetts, until his wife accused him of misconduct with a domestic. Although tried and acquitted by the Church Council, he asked to be dismissed. He became minister of the Congregational church at Chester, Nova Scotia, where his salary was only £20 a year, and he had a very hard time. But he remained in Chester until his death in 1792. He was, of course, not a poet, but he will long be remembered for his humorous verses about the old Harvard College bedmaker.

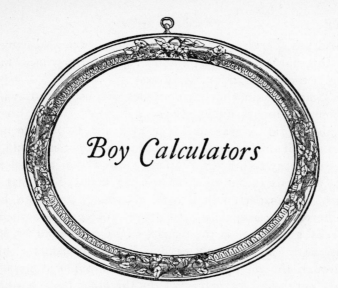

Boy Calculators

I N THE summer of 1812 a sensation was caused in London by the appearance at the Exhibition Rooms in Spring Gardens of an eight-year-old boy mathematical prodigy from New England. This youthful calculator was Zerah Colburn of Cabot, Vermont, a small town near the headwaters of the Onion (now the Winooski) River. A remarkable feature of his case was that the situation of his family in a small town in the heart of Vermont precluded the possibility of his having acquired his powers by the ordinary means of education. It was said of him at the time of his London appearance that without any previous knowledge of the rules of arithmetic, or even of the use and power of Arabic numerals, this miracle child possessed, as if by intuition, the singular faculty of solving a great variety of arithmetical questions by the mere operation of the mind, without the assistance of any visible symbol or contrivance.

In a memoir which he wrote in 1833, a few years before

his death, Zerah Colburn tells of the accidental discovery of this mathematical gift and his rapid rise to fame. Writing in the third person, he says:

"Sometime in the beginning of August, 1810, when about one month under six years of age, being at home, while his father was employed at a joiner's work-bench, Zerah was on the floor, playing in the chips; suddenly he began to say to himself, '5 times 7 are 35—6 times 8 are 48, &c.' His father's attention being arrested by hearing this, so unexpected in a child so young, and who had hitherto possessed no advantages, except perhaps six weeks' attendance at the district school, that summer, left his work, and turning to him began to examine him through the multiplication table; he thought it possible that Zerah had learned this from the other boys, but finding him perfect in the table, his attention was more deeply fixed; and he asked the product of 13 × 97 to which 1261 was instantly given in answer. He now concluded that something unusual had actually taken place; indeed he has often said he should not have been more surprised, if some one had risen up out of the earth and stood erect before him."

Shortly afterward a neighbor rode up and, calling in, was told of the amazing occurrence. He wished to examine the boy, and, having done so, the fact of Zerah's remarkable gift was soon known all over town. Although many were inclined to be skeptical, a personal examination soon convinced them of the truth of the reports. Within a year the story not only traveled throughout the United States but even reached Europe, where both French and English journals commented on the extraordinary case.

"Very soon after the discovery of his remarkable powers," Zerah's account continues, "many gentlemen at

Zerah Colburn

that time possessing influence and public confidence
throughout the state, being made acquainted with the
circumstances, were desirous of having such a course
adopted as might directly lead to a full development of
his talent, and its application to purposes of general utili-
ty. Accordingly Mr. Colburn carried his son to Danville,
to be present during the session of the Court. His child
was very generally seen and questioned by the Judge,
members of the bar, and others. The Legislature of Ver-

mont being about to convene at Montpelier, they were advised to visit that place, which they did in October. Here large numbers had an opportunity of witnessing his calculating powers, and the conclusion was general that such a thing had never been known before. Many questions which were out of the common limits of Arithmetic, were proposed with a view to puzzle him, but he answered them correctly; as for instance—which is the most, twice twenty-five, or twice five and twenty (2 × 25 or 2 × 5 + 20)? Ans.: twice twenty-five. Which is the most, six dozen dozen, or half a dozen dozen (6 × 12 × 12 or 6 × 12)? Ans.: six dozen dozen. It is a fact that somebody asked how many black beans would make five white ones? Ans.: five if you skin them. Thus it appeared that he could not only compute and combine numbers readily, but also he possessed a quickness of thought somewhat uncommon among children, in other things."

Zerah's father exhibited him in various parts of the United States. In Boston, on his first visit in the fall of 1810, the child wonder was asked the number of seconds in 2,000 years. He answered,

730,000 days.
17,520,000 hours.
1,051,200,000 minutes.
63,072,000,000 seconds.

Allowing that a clock strikes 156 times in 1 day, how many times will it strike in 2,000 years? 113,880,000 times.

What is the product of 12,225 multiplied by 1,223? 14,951,175.

What is the square of 1,449? 2,099,601.

Supposing I have a cornfield in which are 7 acres, having 17 rows to each acre, 64 hills to each row, 8 ears on a hill, and 150 kernels on an ear; how many kernels in the cornfield? 9,139,200.

The following June in Portsmouth, New Hampshire, Zerah answered the following questions:

Admitting the distance between Concord and Boston to be 65 miles, how many steps must I take in going this distance, allowing that I go three feet at a step? The answer, 114,400, was given in ten seconds.

How many days and hours since the Christian Era commenced, 1811 years ago? Answered in twenty seconds, 661,015 days, and 15,864,360 hours.

How many seconds in eleven years? Answered in four seconds, 346,896,000.

What sum multiplied by itself will produce 998,001? In less than four seconds, 999.

How many hours in 38 years, 2 months, and 7 days? In six seconds, 334,488.

Everywhere Zerah went he was well received. In several towns various plans were suggested for the education of the boy free of expense to his family. It was felt that a suitable education would greatly extend and improve his wonderful talents and eventually he would shed some light upon those subjects with which his mind seemed peculiarly fitted to deal. But his father decided to take him abroad, and in May, 1812, they arrived in London, where many eminent persons saw and conversed with Zerah and were struck with astonishment at his premature skill in mathematics.

In a prospectus issued at this period, it was said, "He will tell the exact product arising from the multiplication of any number, consisting of two, three, or four figures, by any other number consisting of the like number of figures. Or, any number, consisting of six or seven places of figures, being proposed, he will determine with equal expedition and ease, all the factors of which it is composed. This singular faculty consequently extends not only to the raising of powers, but also to the extraction of the square and cube roots of the number proposed; and likewise to the means of determining whether it be a prime number (or a number incapable of division by any other number); for which case there does not exist, at present, any general rule amongst mathematicians."

In person Zerah Colburn was described as larger and more robust than the generality of children at his age, with a fair complexion and red hair. "In his general disposition he is uncommonly docile and affectionate; but discovers considerable pride of opinion, and is chagrined when detected in an error. He is remarkably inquisitive, and is never satisfied with a superficial examination of any new object or fact. Music seems to excite him most powerfully, and next to this pictures."

The Colburns remained in London about two years and then, after visiting Ireland and Scotland, went to Paris, where for about nine months Zerah was a scholar at the Lycée Napoléon. This continental sojourn proved financially disappointing. Zerah was not the box-office attraction in Paris that he had been in London. He attributed his failure "to the native frivolity and lightness of the people." But the Napoleonic wars, then going full blast, may have had something to do with it.

Early in 1816, after eighteen months in France, Zerah and his father returned to London. By this time they were as poor as a couple of rectory rats, but the Earl of Bristol came to their rescue, and under his patronage Zerah was placed in Westminster School. Here he remained until 1819, when because of his repugnance to the fagging system—the older boys beat the damn Yankee —his father took him from the school.

The elder Colburn urged the boy to go on the stage, but as a last resort Zerah turned to teaching instead. The disappointments and privations of the two proved more than the father could stand, and the harassed man fell a victim to his troubles in 1824.

The difficulties of Mr. Colburn, however, were not a patch on those of his wife. Except for a little money which he had left her to pay some debts on their scrubby farm, he made absolutely no provision for her for twelve years, saddling the poor woman with the responsibility of bringing up seven children, five sons and two daughters, the oldest of whom was only fourteen when her husband and Zerah departed. But by working desperately hard in house and field she managed to keep the family together and eventually to sell out and obtain a better farm. Mr. Colburn was evidently a man of golden dreams who hoped through exploiting Zerah to make a packet of money for himself and his family which would compensate them for the hardships they had undergone. But he was no Barnum, the boy prodigy grew older, and the elder Colburn died penniless.

After paying some of his father's debts, Zerah, now twenty years old, came home. Here he joined the Congregational church but, finding it spiritually uncongenial, turned Methodist and became a minister. For nine years he preached in Vermont and then left the ministry to become professor of languages at Norwich University, a position which he held until his death in 1839. Meanwhile, he married, in 1829, and became the father of six children. His powers of rapid mental calculation remained with him, but not so strongly as in the days of his youth.

In more than one sense Zerah Colburn was very digital. For, in addition to his amazing powers of ready reckoning, he had six toes on each foot. This peculiarity, he said, ran in the Colburn family, his father and two of his brothers having not only a dozen toes apiece but twelve fingers as well. The mark, which could be traced back through a number of generations, made Zerah wonder if he was lineally descended from Philistine blood (see I Chronicles xx, 6). His father's extra fingers were taken off in London by a surgeon who was anxious to remove Zerah's spare toes because of their probable inconvenience to him when learning to dance. But the operation was not performed, and Zerah said his excessive equipment of toes never caused him any trouble. Indeed, the chronicle inclines one to think that he might have made a good tap dancer.

Another boy mathematical wonder who came from Vermont was Truman H. Safford. Born in Royalton in 1836, at the age of twenty-two months he could recite the alphabet, which he taught himself from blocks. When he was six he told his mother that, if she would tell him the distance around their farm in rods, he would give her the measurement in barleycorns. Told that the circumference was 1,040 rods, he concentrated for a few moments and answered 617,760 barleycorns.

When young Safford was not yet ten he computed an almanac for Bradford, Vermont, for 1846, and the following year not only for Bradford but also for Boston, Philadelphia, and Cincinnati. At this time he could solve in his mind in a minute or two examples in algebra, mensuration, and trigonometry. Astronomy interested the boy deeply.

Reverend George Denison, a professor in Kenyon College, while visiting relatives in Royalton, examined the young marvel. "I believe him to surpass anything on record in the history of man," declared the professor, "and to open a door by which we are permitted to see something of what our minds are, and what they can become when this natural body shall have been exchanged for the spiritual."

As the boy's fame spread, many persons through curiosity or skepticism as to his precocity wanted to test him. Despite the lad's frailty and nervousness, the Reverend Henry W. Adams, the agent of the American Bible Society, put him through a third degree lasting three hours that left the boy nearly exhausted. The final request this reverend inquisitor made of the child was to give the result of multiplying 365, 365, 365, 365, 365, by itself.

Another minister present in the torture chamber reported afterward in the *Ladies Repository,* "He flew around the room like a top, pulled his pantaloons over his boots, bit his hand, rolled his eyes in their sockets, and then [seemed] to be in agony, until, in not more than one minute," he had the correct answer. "The boy looked pale and said he was tired. He said it was the largest sum he ever did." This multiplying was one of Zerah Colburn's star feats.

The boy's parents had sense enough to put a stop to his being subjected to ordeals of this kind, nor would they consent to his being exploited. In 1847, President Edward Everett of Harvard and Professor Benjamin Peirce became interested in young Safford. They persuaded the Saffords to sell their Vermont farm and move to Cambridge, where their son could prepare for college under proper supervision.

It was at this point in young Safford's career, according

to Evelyn M. W. Lovejoy, the historian of Royalton, Vermont, that James Russell Lowell wrote a facetious letter to a friend about the boy, which the friend was tactless enough to print. Lowell promptly wrote to the father apologizing for the letter, which, he said, was more hurtful to himself than to anybody else.

After his graduation from Harvard in 1854, Truman Safford spent twelve years at the Harvard Observatory. In 1866 he was made director of the Dearborn Observatory and Professor of Astronomy at the University of Chicago. Lack of support of the observatory following the Chicago fire of 1871 made it necessary for him to look for another job. For the next five years he was connected with various United States government surveys. In 1876, this bearded, keen-eyed man was made Professor of Astronomy at Williams College, a position which he held until his death in 1901.

Overstrain is said to have impaired his intellectual gifts somewhat, but his powers were nevertheless remarkable. Astronomers, like artists, develop quickness of vision, and Truman Safford could take things in at a glance. Looking for a particular book in a library he could stand back from the shelves and spot it in a flash. And once he took up a book he could tear the heart out of it in no time. President Carter of Williams said in his funeral address, "He came nearer to Goethe's claim that by reading one page in a book he could tell all that there was in it, than anyone I have ever known."

Like Zerah Colburn, Truman Safford never disclosed the method he used in making lightning calculations. Apparently both of these Vermont mathematical wizards had to keep in practice or they suffered loss of speed.

Body Snatchers

IN THE spring of 1818 the following notice was printed in a Massachusetts newspaper:

"$500 DOLLARS REWARD

"Most daring and sacrilegious Robbery.

"STOLEN from the grave yard in Chebacco Parish in Ipswich, the bodies of eight persons, seven of whom were interred since the 13th of October last; the other, a coloured man, about six years ago. As without doubt they have all, ere this time, passed under the dissecting knife of the anatomist, either of the rude novice in the art or the skilled professor, little hope is entertained of recovering any relict of them for the consolation of the deeply afflicted friends. But whoever will give any information of this atrocious villainy, so as to detect and bring to justice, either the traders in this abominable traffic, or their in-

human employers, shall receive the above reward; and
the thanks of an afflicted and distressed people.

"William Andrews jun.

Thomas Choate

Nathan Burnham

"Committee.

"Ipswich, Chebacco Parish,
"April 25th, 1818."

Prior to 1830 proper legal provision was not made in
Massachusetts for supplying students of anatomy with
human bodies for dissection, and yet the law required persons who aspired to be doctors to be versed in anatomy.
There were few medical schools in those days, and, if a
student could not afford to attend one, he studied medicine
with an established physician, just as one learned to be
a lawyer by reading law in an attorney's office. The doctor
gave the student private lessons in anatomy and let him
serve as his assistant when he called on his patients. One
physician of great reputation near Worcester used to have
from a dozen to eighteen young men studying with him
at one time, all of whom were cloaked and hatted alike
and all rode horseback. The doctor himself, superbly
mounted and elegantly dressed in a great wig, a cocked
hat, and cloak, cut a gallant figure as he galloped about
the countryside at the head of his cavalcade of students.

Under the old Massachusetts law, judges sitting in capital cases could order the bodies of executed criminals
turned over to the surgeons for anatomical purposes, but
the gallows as a source of supply proved wholly inade-
quate, and students were of necessity obliged to dig up
bodies for themselves, or purchase them from muddy-
booted Jerry Crunchers. The law, strangely enough, seems

to have tolerated body snatching, for it permitted doctors to have dead human bodies in their possession for scientific purposes without having to answer embarrassing questions as to how they came by them.

The public, of course, looked upon the activities of the resurrectionists with horror, loathing, and indignation. Stealing bodies was quite bad enough, but the method used made it seem especially wicked. The resurrectionists seldom bothered to open a grave fully, but simply dug a hole down to the head of the coffin, which was broken open, and, after affixing a hook at the end of a rope under the chin of the dead person, fished the body out through the hole. It was a heartless business, and many wild stories were told of the body snatchers.

When, a few years after the affair at Ipswich, proposals were made to establish the Berkshire Medical College at Pittsfield, the people of that town had grave misgivings. They were not unmindful of the benefits of having such an institution located in their town, but they feared the body-snatching tendencies of the students. Pittsfield was not near any large city from which bodies might be obtained with little likelihood of any questions being raised, and it was said that there was not a village graveyard in Berkshire County which had escaped the visitations of the resurrectionists. Nor were matters helped when it was learned that the plan called for locating the school in an old hotel conveniently situated next to the central burying ground. Only a short time before, Pittsfield had been deeply stirred by an outrageous case of body snatching within its limits.

Every objection to the plan, however, was overcome, and the college was established. Dissecting rooms were provided in the hotel stables, and during the forty-four

years of its existence Berkshire Medical College graduated 1,138 students. In his *History of Pittsfield* (1876),
J. E. A. Smith devotes a chapter to this interesting institution, reviewing in detail the body-snatching side of
its story. From this source I have derived the following
particulars.

In 1820, only two years before the founding of the
Medical College, Pittsfield was thrown into a state of
seething excitement by the discovery that the body of
George Butler, Jr., a young man of respectable family
with numerous relatives, had been stolen from its grave.
Young Butler died in November, 1819, and during the
following winter his mother repeatedly dreamed that his
grave was empty. This may, perhaps, be accounted for by
the fact that suspicion had been aroused in the fall by the
appearance of the sod and the finding of a shroud sleeve
in the burial ground, although it is not known that she
was told these facts. In any case, when at her request one
of her surviving sons early in May opened his brother's
grave, and found that the body had indeed been removed
in the usual rough manner, the mother's dream conspired
with other circumstances to deepen the public horror. Almost every person in Pittsfield, young and old alike, as
well as many from neighboring towns, went to gaze, shud-
dering, into the gaping grave, which was purposely left
open all summer, exposing its shattered and tenantless
coffin, to remind the spectator of the shocking circumstances of its desecration.

A special town meeting was called on June 7 to consider the case, and to see what measures should be taken
to prevent in future "the horrid and savage practice" of
body snatching. At this meeting a committee reported that,
while they "viewed with abhorrence, the violations of the

right of sepulcher," they could find no statute of the Commonwealth regarding such an offense, and that, in their opinion, the town had no power to levy a tax for the purpose of offering a reward for the detection of the perpetrators. The offenders might, however, be indicted for a misdemeanor at common law, if they could be detected by the activity and vigilance of private citizens. Somewhat astounded by this exposition of the law, the town instructed the selectmen to "lay the facts before the governor and council, and request them to take such order thereon as they might deem proper;" but, if they did so, it had no effect, for the first Massachusetts statute for the protection of the repose of the dead was not passed until 1830.

The town further appointed a committee of twelve to collect money for the purpose of offering a reward for the detection of any person who had robbed or might violate any grave in the town. It also directed Josiah Bissell, whose store adjoined the central burial ground, to keep an eye on the place and from time to time inspect it to see whether there were any indications that it had been disturbed.

In 1822, with these facts still fresh in the public mind, it was with good reason that the trustees of the Medical College in their first circular endeavored to allay the fears naturally aroused by the location of their institution. "That repose of the dead had been disturbed" they did not deny; but such outrages, they pointed out, had arisen chiefly from lack of a seminary where students could pursue anatomical researches. Compelled by law to obtain a complete knowledge of anatomy, and unable to meet the expense of city schools, students were driven to expedients as repugnant to their own feelings as they were odious

to the public. The new school, therefore, increased rather
than diminished the security of the graveyards.

At the same time the trustees showed consideration
for the feelings of "those many individuals of excellent
minds who entertained prejudices against the dissection
of the human frame" at all, and suggested for their peace
of mind "that the great number of anatomical preparations in the museum lessened the necessity for extensive
dissection." They even went so far as to add that "comparative anatomy, or the dissection of brute animals, furnished a substitute for the use of the human body, which
would be neither overlooked nor neglected." Which looks,
remarks the Pittsfield historian, very much as if the venerable fathers in medicine were attempting to soothe
their fellow citizens with opiates of very questionable or-
thodoxy. He suspected that all the dissection of dumb animals which was ever done or contemplated in the institution was witnessed in no more solemn amphitheater than
the dining hall. The trustees, however, declared that, as
the state imposed upon them the duty of providing the
means of instructions in every department, including anatomy, they would faithfully perform that duty, although
"with a most sacred regard to private feeling as well as
to public sensibility."

While thus addressing the public, the trustees endeavored to show their good faith by stringent provisions in
the college statutes requiring the faculty to procure their
subjects for dissection only from the largest cities; that
no student should be concerned in obtaining them; that
no private dissection by students should be permitted, and
that any who might infringe this rule should be publicly
exposed. These bylaws, however, did not perfectly accomplish their purpose, says Mr. Smith.

It is probable that the graveyards in the immediate vicinity of the college were safer for its establishment, and, perhaps, as a large number of anatomical students could avail themselves of the same subjects, and some of these were bought by the faculty in the large cities, where traffic in human bodies was carried on with more or less freedom, there were not so many illegally obtained in the neighborhood as before. But there were frequent and generally credited reports of the desecration of burial grounds in towns at some distance from Pittsfield by the students of the Berkshire Medical College.

Finally, a party of students was followed from the eastern part of Hampden County, and a body which they had stolen was recovered at Westfield. In the early part of March, 1830, the bodies of two persons who had just been buried at Montague and Conway were found to have been disinterred and were traced to two students of the college, who were arrested. The bodies were speedily recovered without mutilation and restored to their friends. The pursuers found the warmest sympathy among the people of Pittsfield, who in the height of their indignation, before legal measures proved effective, threatened to take the law into their own hands. Major Butler Goodrich, a local warhorse, even offered to head a party to demolish the college buildings unless the ghastly prey of the students was surrendered.

A full town meeting was held on March 7, in which the citizens as usual expressed their "sentiments of unmingled indignation and horror" and pledged the town's "best endeavors to aid in the discovery of persons residing among or near us who have been charged with this foul offense; and to place a social ban upon those who were known to be guilty, but who from the difficulty of obtaining direct evidence might escape legal punishment." Acknowledging the necessity of dissection, they held all medical institutions to a strict responsibility in regard to the manner of obtaining subjects, and declared that those permitting students to provide subjects for themselves or the college ought to be discountenanced and held up to "public censure and public shame." Jonathan Allen, a trustee of the Medical College, was moderator of the meeting which passed these resolutions.

In another case preserved by tradition the result of the pursuit was not so satisfactory. The officers and friends of the deceased were permitted to search the college buildings; but were accompanied by a tall student who is alleged to have concealed the body of the subject, a slight girl emaciated by long illness, under one of the long camlet cloaks then in fashion.

This last grim story the Pittsfield historian admits does not rest on the most unimpeachable testimony; but he says it is likely enough to have been true, and, even if false, its very invention illustrates the popular feeling.

In still another case a person who was employed in a local factory, having died, was buried in the northeast corner of the old graveyard, but when friends from a distance came to disinter and remove the body, it was found that others had visited the grave before them and snatched it. This affair stirred up the customary excitement, which was heightened by a ludicrous incident. One of the mourning friends, resorting too often to the tavern for consolation, became intoxicated and fell on his face in the open grave, whereupon a student bystander proposed to leave him to fill the vacancy which he had discovered. The jester, however, came near being rewarded for his ill-timed pleasantry by being placed there himself.

Despite its splendid record, the Berkshire Medical College became a casualty of the Civil War. There had been a constant financial struggle from the beginning to keep the place going, and the war proved the last straw. The institution was closed not long after Lincoln's death, and its property was finally sold in 1871. Its body-snatching problems were typical of those of other early New England medical schools.

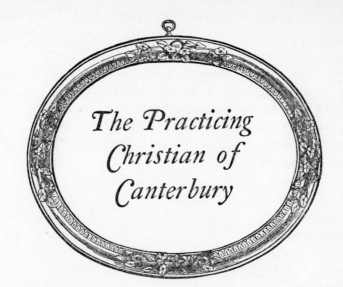

The Practicing
Christian of
Canterbury

CONNECTICUT's Canterbury tale needs no varnishing. The plain facts speak for themselves and sufficiently plead the case of the story's lone heroine, Prudence Crandall.

Prudence was a good-looking Quaker girl from Rhode Island, with wavy hair that sprang alive from a good forehead, and a round vivid face with soft regular features. Born in Hopkinton, Rhode Island, September 3, 1803, she took up teaching as a career, soon winning for herself "a high reputation as a female instructress."

In the autumn of 1831, Prudence suggested to the leading families of Canterbury, a prosperous community in the eastern part of Connecticut, not far from the Rhode Island line, that she open a boarding school for girls in the town. Conditions favored the establishment of such an institution, and her proposal met with immediate approval. A large, comfortable house near the green in the center of Canterbury was obtained, and the school was opened at once.

The first year all went well. The girls and their parents were pleased. The future success of the institution seemed assured. But the following autumn the outlook became somewhat overcast.

In September, 1831, a respectable colored girl named Sarah Harris, who lived in Canterbury and was a member of the Congregational church, wishing to qualify herself as teacher among people of her own race, applied for admission to the school. Miss Crandall hesitated, but when Sarah Harris came to her again and repeated her request, very earnestly pleading to be admitted, the Quaker headmistress decided to take her as a pupil. When the parents of the white students learned this they were greatly perturbed. It was strongly intimated to Miss Crandall that unless she dismissed Sarah Harris the school would be ruined.

Prudence Crandall had admitted Sarah Harris because she thought it was her religious duty to do so. To her it appeared unjust and oppressive to discriminate against a worthy person on account of that person's color. She believed that Christian precepts demanded justice for all, and a spirit willing to make sacrifices for others. Fortified with these convictions, she gave her answer to the white patrons of her seminary.

"The school may sink," she said, "but I will not give up Sarah Harris."

Fully realizing the consequences of the stand she had taken, Prudence sought the advice of persons who were interested in the advancement of the colored people. The same year she opened her school, public opinion had been stirred by the publication of William Lloyd Garrison's uncompromising antislavery paper, *The Liberator,* and the great abolitionist editor was one of the persons she consulted. After her return to Canterbury, and carefully considering the whole matter, particularly the deep prejudice that existed against Negroes and the difficulties which they encountered when seeking an education, she decided to open a school for their benefit. Accordingly, she dismissed all her white students, and at the same time announced that on April 1 she would conduct her school for "young ladies and little misses of color."

Canterbury was shaken out of its featherbed complacency. The people were alarmed lest such a school should draw what they considered an undesirable class of persons to the town. The presence of a lot of Negroes in the center of Canterbury was to them intolerable. A town meeting was held March 9 to consider the matter, and a committee was appointed to call on Miss Crandall to persuade her to abandon her plan.

"It will lead to intermarriage," the town fathers told her, "and a general leveling of society."

"Moses had a black wife," she answered.

All efforts to stop her failed, and the school was duly opened with twenty colored students. Canterbury promptly declared war. Storekeepers refused to sell anything to the school, the trustees of the church would let none of them attend worship, the young misses of color were assailed and reviled whenever they appeared in public. The local doctor did not dare attend any sick person at the school. Prudence Crandall herself was threatened with violence. It was enough to frighten any girl, but she did not falter. A church in a neighboring town opened its doors to Miss Crandall and her girls, and apparently there was no suffering during the siege from a lack of sup-

plies, though it was serious when the school well was de-
filed with filth. The situation was one that gave full scope
to the meanness and nastiness of the small-town mind. No
one in Canterbury seems to have had the courage to con-
demn the disgraceful things that were done to break up the
school.

Canterbury. The school is at the left.

An old law relating to vagrants was unearthed which
provided that any person who failed to leave town after
being warned by the selectmen to get out should be
"whipped on the naked body." Laws of this kind were
common throughout New England, and the town records
are full of such warnings. They were aimed at mounte-
banks, wandering fiddlers, gypsies, medicine men, wild
girls, and all undesirable persons. A warrant warning one
of Miss Crandall's students, a pretty seventeen-year-old
from Providence, to leave Canterbury was issued under the

old law, but the girl could not be frightened into leaving.

The next move made by the Canterburians was to petition the legislature to pass an act that would enable the town to abolish the school. On May 24 a law was enacted prohibiting the instruction of colored persons from other states in any schools, except in the free common schools and incorporated academies of the state, without the consent of the town in which such school should be located. Since most of Prudence Crandall's students were from out of the state, the statute was thought to provide the people of Canterbury with an implement of legal warfare that would enable them to shut down the school. News of the passage of this law was celebrated in Canterbury by the ringing of the church bell and the firing of cannon.

A few weeks later proceedings under the new law were begun against Prudence Crandall. She was arrested and jailed in the adjoining town of Brooklyn. Her sympathizers were shocked when they heard she was confined in a cell that had just been occupied by a condemned murderer. But she was imprisoned for only about a day before being released on bail to appear before the Superior Court.

Although the people of Canterbury now believed that it would not be long before they would be rid of Prudence and her brood, there was no letup in the molestations to which she and her students were subjected. On one of the school exhibition days four little misses of color sang a special hymn that ended with the lines:

But we forgive, forgive the men who persecute us so;
May God in mercy save their souls from everlasting
  woe.

Prudence Crandall, though she may have lacked friends in Canterbury, had plenty outside. Prominent Abolitionists rallied to her support, providing the best legal counsel procurable for her defense, and a paper was launched in Connecticut to present her case. Public interest in the controversy was widespread.

The first round of the legal contest was a draw. The jury was deadlocked, and no verdict was reached. Preparations were made immediately for a second trial. At this trial the constitutionality of the statute which Prudence Crandall was alleged to have broken was argued, her counsel contending that the law violated the constitutional provision, "The citizens of each state shall be entitled to all the privileges and immunities of citizens in the several states." The trial judge ruled that Negroes were not citizens. Prudence Crandall was convicted, and her case was appealed to the Supreme Court of Connecticut.

In July, 1834, the Supreme Court handed down its decision. It did not pass on the constitutional question which had been raised, but, avoiding that issue, reversed the finding of the lower court on the ground of insufficient evidence. News of the court's decision was not greeted in Canterbury by the ringing of the church bell and the firing of cannon.

The siege of the school had now lasted nearly a year and a half. Prudence's sister, Almira, had come to help her, but things grew steadily worse. A mob attacked the school at midnight armed with clubs and iron bars. Doors and windows were smashed and the house set on fire. Luckily the fire was quickly extinguished, but the situation was now too dangerous for Prudence to cope with, and she was at last convinced of the hopelessness of trying to carry on her school in Canterbury. So it was disbanded in September.

Visitors to Canterbury may still see the mansion in which the Quaker schoolteacher and her "young ladies and little misses of color" held out bravely against impossible odds.

On the breaking up of her school, Prudence married the Reverend Calvin Philleo, a Baptist minister from Ithaca, New York, and moved first to New York State, then to Illinois. She became an advocate of women's causes. After her husband's death many years later, she went to Kansas to live with her brother, Hezekiah Crandall. She lived to be a very old lady, dying at Elk Falls, Kansas, January 28, 1889.

Conscience pricked Connecticut to atonement. Shortly after the Civil War a generous pension was granted to her for life. So much, bare justice required.

The Old Leather Man

AMONG the waxworks in the famous old Eden Musée in New York there used to be the figure of the Old Leather Man of Connecticut, dressed in the actual leather garments which he wore on his journeys through Connecticut. There are people living today who remember this strange traveler, who for twenty-seven years, from 1862 to 1889, was a familiar sight to the inhabitants of the towns along his route, which he followed restlessly summer and winter, regardless of the weather. Many persons could with perfect truth repeat the lines of the old nursery rhyme—

> One misty, moisty morning,
> When cloudy was the weather,
> I chanced to meet an old man
> Clothed all in leather.

The crazy costume which gave the Old Leather Man his name consisted of a crudely-fashioned leather cap with a visor, like a railroad conductor's, and a patchwork suit made of dozens of pieces of black leather of different shapes and sizes, cut mostly from the tops of high, old-fashioned boots, such as countrymen used to wear, and for the conditioning of which a special pan of grease was kept on the shelf in most farmhouse kitchens. These odds and ends of leather were not sewed together neatly, but were laced coarsely with leather thongs half an inch wide. The work was well done, but the seams were not tight, and while this gave ventilation in summer, at other times it admitted the wind and the rain. As it was not until the latter part of his career that the Old Leather Man wore anything under his leaky outfit, his own hide must have acquired the toughness of leather. The footgear in which he annually walked between three and four thousand miles was a roughly-made pair of high leather moccasins into which he tucked his leather breeches. Also of his own making were the leather mittens that he wore in cold weather.

These mittens and his leather haversack are in the possession of the Connecticut Historical Society. The sack, which is about the size of a postman's bag, is made of a dozen or fifteen miscellaneous pieces of leather held together with thongs. It was probably in this bag that he carried his iron spider, his tin pail, and his hatchet, reserving the cloth bag, which he also carried, for his jackknife, awl, and other small tools and articles, which would have slipped out through the gaps in the leather bag. With his quaint luggage and his staff and his queer garb, the Old Leather Man presented as strange an appearance as any wayfarer ever to plod the byways of New England.

The circuit which he made measured 366 miles, two-thirds of it in Connecticut, the rest in New York. This circuit he completed regularly every thirty-four days, reaching a given point on his route at the same time on each round. At Forestville, Connecticut, the day and hour when he would emerge from the woods and come down the Burlington road were foretold accurately time and again. In 1884 and 1885 he was observed as he made nineteen consecutive passages. His starting point was Harwinton, Connecticut, and if for any reason he was delayed along the way, he cut short the New York end of his journey in order to begin his schedule on time.

The Old Leather Man's itinerary was determined by Chauncey L. Hotchkiss of Forestville, who not only traced his course but also noted the places where he had caves. The towns through which the Old Leather Man passed were Harwinton (cave), Berlin, Meriden, Middlefield, Middletown, Durham, Haddam, Chester, Essex, Saybrook, Westbrook, Killingworth, Clinton, Madison, Guilford (cave), Orange, Milford, Stratford, North Bridgeport, Fairfield, Westport, Norwalk, New Canaan (cave), Wilton, New York State Line, Purdy Station, Kensico, Croton Falls, Doanesville, Brewster, East Peekskill, Yorktown, Shrub Oak Plains, Turkey Mountain (cave), Sawmill Valley Woods, New Fairfield, New Milford, Bridgewater, Roxbury, Woodbury, Watertown (cave), Thomaston, Plymouth, and then to Harwinton again.

This route—240 miles in Connecticut and 126 miles in New York—could be covered in a month by the Old Leather Man tramping twelve miles a day. It took him a little longer than this because he made it a practice to spend two days in Guilford, where he built himself a hut of railroad ties on a hillside. Here he made repairs to his leather outfit. Once in Woodbury he permitted a tanner to oil his creaky suit.

But who was the Old Leather Man, and what furious

fancy drove him round and round in a circle, month after month, year after year, like some ancient Tom o'Bedlam? And why the leather suit which he might have exchanged without disadvantage for the tatters of a scarecrow? Although the Old Leather Man attracted much attention and aroused great interest, very little is actually known about him, or the reasons for his nomadism.

He was neither a peddler nor a beggar. He would never take money directly, but he did accept food from persons he knew were friendly to him, and would pick up small change obviously left for him. For over a quarter of a century a house near New Haven was one of his regular ports of call. He never smiled and seldom spoke to anyone, not even to express his gratitude for food or favors bestowed on him. When he did speak it was in broken English in a mild and gentle tone surprising in so rough-looking a character. Tradition says he was trilingual, speaking French, German, and English. He was thought to be French, and seemed pleased when addressed in his native tongue, but even then remained uncommunicative. Around his neck he wore a tiny crucifix, and in his pack he carried a French prayer book printed in 1814. Once he was seen reading in a cave in Woodbury, but not in his prayer book. He was absorbed in a newspaper.

Inevitably romantic stories were invented to account for his strange manner of life. Disappointment in love is the stock reason given in all such cases, and it was the one put forward in the case of the Old Leather Man. The mildly distracted old fellow was said to be Jules Bourglay, the son of a woodcarver of Lyons, France. He was employed in the leather trade and fell in love with his employer's daughter, whom it was said he would have married if he had not made a serious business error which ruined his prospective father-in-law and postponed indefinitely his own plans to mate with the girl. This disaster unhinged his mind, and for a year he was in an institution. He then disappeared, and his whereabouts were unknown until he turned up in this country. When he was discovered, his relatives attempted to induce him to return to France, but he refused and took to the road and to wearing a leather suit as a penance. Such in brief is the commonly accepted story of the Old Leather Man, which a Philadelphia lady claimed was plagiarized from a work of fiction which she wrote before he died. The whole Jules Bourglay story, she said, was her invention.

Another story is that he was an old colored man and a fugitive from justice, one of a gang of whites and Negroes, who many years ago had their rendezvous at a notorious resort near New Hartford. This thieves' kitchen, which was called the Barkhampstead Lighthouse because there was always a light there at night, was broken up by the authorities after many crimes had been committed in the region. Two photographs of the Old Leather Man which I have seen show a strong, sturdy person of medium height who might easily have passed for a Negro, but actually he seems to have been just a grimy old man, with whom, I am told, it was well not to get within odorous proximity. The suggestion that he was a fugitive from justice is not one in which any confidence can be placed. His terrifying appearance—to children he was a bogey—made many people think he was a dangerous character, but, if he had been wanted, it would have been easy to apprehend him. If he fled from anything, it was from something more perplexing and torturing than justice. The only time he seems to have fallen into the hands of the authorities was about a year before his death, when an agent of the Connecticut Humane Society, seeing that he was suffering from cancer of the lip, took him to a hospital. In March, 1889, he was found dead in a cave near Ossining, New York.

The Old Leather Man was typical of a class of tramps once not uncommon in New England. Several even dressed in leather, and used the Old Leather Man's title, but none presented quite so eccentric an appearance as the original Old Leather Man himself. It is possible that his remarkable suit may still be in existence. The wax figures from the old Eden Musée in New York were taken to Coney Island in 1918, and may have survived the fire which swept the resort in 1932. Inquiry among the waxwork showmen might yield news of the outfit which gave name and fame to the Old Leather Man of Connecticut.

Nantucket Folk

ALTHOUGH a very general prejudice formerly existed among the people living in the hinterland of New England against the inhabitants of Cape Cod, no such feeling was felt by the mainlanders for the people of Nantucket. Distance seems to have given the place and the people a certain measure of enchantment. To the rest of New England, Nantucket, lying twenty miles off in the mist to the southward of Cape Cod, appeared to be a little world by itself, with interests, pursuits, and a manner of existence all its own.

The fact that during the Revolution the Nantucket Quakers tried to remain aloof from the conflict was not held against them for long. They were in a bad spot and suffered dreadfully. At the outbreak of hostilities in 1775, Nantucket had one hundred and fifty vessels employing 2,200 men on whaling voyages. By the end of the war the whale fleet had been reduced to thirty vessels, and 1,200 men had been killed or captured. Completely at the mercy

of the British navy, the islanders' supplies from the mainland were cut to the barest necessities, lest provisions fall
into the hands of the enemy, who plundered them shamelessly. So impoverished did they become that one year no
taxes were levied.

They had barely recovered from this setback when the
War of 1812 broke out. With the memory of their losses
and sufferings in the Revolution still in mind, and knowing that they must continue to kill whales or starve, it is
not surprising that on August 31, 1814, Nantucket declared itself neutral. But again the islanders were nearly
ruined; the whaling fleet was reduced to a skeleton, and
many Nantucketers went to Davy Jones or became prisoners of John Bull.

In connection with the prisoners of war, it is interesting to recall a story told of Sir Isaac Coffin, the Boston-
born British admiral who was related to the Coffin family
of Nantucket. One day during the war Sir Isaac visited
Dartmoor Prison for the purpose of releasing any American prisoner bearing his family name. Among those who
presented themselves was a Negro.

"Ah," said Sir Isaac, "you a Coffin, too?"

"Yes, massa."

"How old are you?"

"Me thirty years, massa."

"Well, then, you are not one of the Coffins, for they
never turn black until forty."

Despite the Nantucketers' attempt to sit on the fence
during the war, New Englanders generally respected and
admired the hardy inhabitants of this offshore town, whose
success in the dangerous nautical adventure of whaling was
a matter of regional pride. A mainland author, writing
of life on the island in a popular geographical work pub-

lished in Boston some years later, said, "Nantucket is a happy settlement; not that it has precious metals in its bosom, or fertility in its soil, but because the people are simple, innocent, and contented. . . . The vices of commercial places are hardly known, and it is admitted all

Siasconset, Nantucket

over New England to be a presumption in favor of a man's honesty, that he comes from Nantucket. The Friends or Quakers give to the language a simplicity of diction truly Doric; and, though they take some liberties with the Commonwealth's English, yet to speak in a more classic manner, would be held to savor of affectation and pretension, in a person brought up among them. The various relationships, and the kindly feelings, have introduced the custom of calling elderly people uncle or aunt, and the younger, cousin. Even a stranger falls into this habit. The people generally marry young, and few live in celibacy. They are social to a great degree, and are eminently distinguished for their frequent visitings to sup at each other's houses. They live more as though they made a large family, than a small community."

But how did the islanders feel about the mainlanders? The people of Nantucket have always been a proud island race. A person not a resident of the island was called a foreigner, and such a person is still spoken of as an off-islander. The story is told of a Nantucket schoolboy whose task it was to write about Napoleon. He said, "Napoleon was a great man and a great soldier, but he was an off-islander." The islanders, however, have never been intolerant of the mainlanders. Their courtesy to strangers has been unfailing.

It was apparent from the beginning, when Thomas Macy of Salisbury, Massachusetts, bought Nantucket Island for £30 and two beaver hats in behalf of himself and a few of his fellow townsmen, that the destiny of anyone living there was bound up with the sea. Macy was the first white settler. He went there in 1659 to get away from the Quaker persecutions of the Massachusetts Bay government. Others soon followed him, people with such familiar Nantucket names as Folger, Starbuck, Coffin, Gardner, Coleman, Bunker, and Hussey. There were three thousand Indians living on Nantucket at the time, but by 1700 disease had reduced their numbers to less than four hundred, while the white population had increased to more than eight hundred. Both whites and Indians were dependent on the sea for their livelihood.

"In the year 1690," says Obed Macy in his history of Nantucket, "some persons were on a hill observing the whales spouting and sporting with each other, when one observed; there—pointing to the sea—is a green pasture where our children's grand-children will go for bread."

That year marked the beginning of the whale fishery at Nantucket. The settlers had been on the island long enough to realize that the soil was not well suited to agriculture, and with whales playing about close at hand it was only natural that the islanders should turn to whaling. Killing whales offered better returns than catching mackerel and cod. So Ichabod Paddock of Cape Cod was invited to come to the island to instruct the people in the art of killing whales from the shore in boats. This professor of the harpoon soon taught them the craft, and in no time at all the Nantucketers were bringing home the blubber. The Indians, too, proved apt pupils, improving their own primitive technique in taking whales. Lookouts were set up along the southern side of the island and watchmen posted, who, when one of them sighted a whale in his sector, gave the signal which meant "There she blows." If the men who went out in row boats got their whale, they towed it to port, cut it up, and the blubber was "tried" or boiled in the tryhouse on shore. Whales were plentiful, and the industry, conducted on a co-operative basis with each man getting his part of the kill, flourished.

This system of whaling continued for about twenty-five years, until an incident occurred that resulted in a change of method. Christopher Hussey, one of the original settlers, while beating along the coast in his vessel was blown out to sea, where he chanced upon a sperm whale, the species that produces the best oil. He killed it and returned home in triumph. It was the first sperm whale taken by a Nantucket whaleman, or, so far as is known, by an American. This was in the year 1712. Within a few years the Nantucketers, instead of waiting for the whales to come to them, were pursuing them at sea. This was done in small vessels of from thirty to fifty tons. The whales were cut up where they were killed, but the chunks of blubber were brought back to be "tried" on shore. Returning to port every time a whale was taken was unsatisfactory, especially when a school or pod of whales was encountered, so larger vessels were built equipped with tryworks, and the oil was boiled out at sea. This enabled the whale ships to range farther from home, as was becoming increasingly necessary. By 1760 the whales had largely left the coast, and the era of long voyages began.

These voyages lasted two or three years or more. One captain about to leave port on a voyage was reminded that he hadn't kissed his wife good-by.

"Why should I?" he said. "I am only going to be gone two years."

Many Nantucket whalemen spent most of their lives at sea. Captain Gardner figured that in thirty-seven years he had spent only four years and eight months at home. Two Nantucket captains who were brothers did not see each other for twenty-three years. When whale ships met at sea and the crews visited each other it was called "gamming." Although absent from home for years, the whalers often came to anchor, and the men landed on some tropic island to stretch their legs or went ashore in a foreign port for a frolic.

An English naval officer once challenged a Yankee skipper in a Pacific port, but when the whaleman chose harpoons for weapons the Englishman backed out.

James T. Fields made famous the story of the Nantucket skipper who claimed that he could tell exactly where his ship was solely by the color and taste of the lead after a sounding had been taken. On one voyage his mate, Marden, decided to play a joke on him, and took along some dirt from the parsnip bed of a neighbor in Nantucket. One morning off Cape Horn Marden greased the lead and smeared it with this Nantucket dirt. He then woke the captain and showed it to him.

> The skipper stormed, and tore his hair,
>   Hauled on his boots, and roared to Marden,
> "Nantucket's sunk, and here we are
>   Right over old Marm Hackett's garden!"

The whale ships first ventured around Cape Horn in the 1790's, but it was not until 1820 that they went as far as the coast of Japan. A Nantucket youth who had not doubled the Cape or harpooned a whale could not hope to win a Nantucket girl. There is a tradition that the girls of the island had a secret society the members of which were pledged not to marry a man until he had harpooned a whale. Proud, indeed, was the Nantucket lad who could say he had struck a whale. One of the old Nantucket songs quoted by the author of *Moby Dick* has this refrain:

> So be cheery, my lads, let your hearts never fail
> While the bold harpooner is striking the whale!

The antique Nantucket novel, *Miriam Coffin, or the Whale Fisherman,* is a salty tale about a girl who tells her two suitors that they must go on a whaling voyage and she will marry the more successful one of the two. Neither is fitted for such an undertaking. One is a minister, and the other is no better qualified for chasing whales; but they both go to sea just the same, leaving Miriam to await the outcome. The minister loses his life; the other returns after a lapse of several years. But instead of marrying Miriam, he tells her that before leaving Nantucket he had decided that a girl who could make the fatuous condition to marriage she had proposed was not one he could ever make his wife. And there the novel ends.

It used to be said that the difference between a Cape Cod girl and a Nantucket lass was that a Cape Cod girl when kissed always turned the other cheek, saying, "You darsent do that again," whereas a Nantucket girl would say, "Sheer off, or I'll split your mainsail with a typhoon."

By 1822 the town of Nantucket had so far recovered from the War of 1812 that it had eighty-eight whaling vessels averaging three hundred tons each. In 1828, Daniel Webster, speaking in the United States Senate on the application for the erection of a breakwater at Nantucket, said, "Nantucket itself is a very striking and peculiar portion of the National interest. There is a population of eight or nine thousand persons, living here in the sea, adding largely every year to the National wealth by the boldest and most persevering industry."

There is no doubt that the Nantucket whalemen were the best sailors afloat. Yet whaling was a gamble, and while the profits of a voyage were frequently from $30,000 to $50,000 or more, a ship might return clean instead of greasy. It was also one of the most hazardous occupations, but the seamanship of the crews was so good that the insurance rate on a Nantucket whaler was half that on an English one.

In battling with a whale, small boats were frequently upset or smashed and lives lost. Three cases are known of a ship's being sunk by a whale, a fate that overtook the *Essex* of Nantucket in the Pacific Ocean on November 13, 1820. The ship was then in the midst of a school of whales, and three boats were launched. Shortly after a young whale had been taken, another of mammoth proportions, supposed to have been its mother, collided violently with the ship and did some damage. It then tried to get a grip on the *Essex* with its jaws but, failing in this, withdrew. When about a quarter of a mile away, it turned and swam with tremendous power and speed directly toward the ship. It struck head on with such violence that the vessel was not only stopped dead but forced to give way. The impact flattened every man on deck. The bluff bows of the *Essex* were completely crumpled. The ship immediately filled and sank.

The members of the crew in the three whaleboats decided to steer for the Marquesas Islands. Sails were rigged, and they set out together, but soon became separated. Two of the boats were picked up, one with three men alive, by a British vessel; the other, with only two survivors who had been in the boat three months, by a Nantucket ship. The third whaleboat was never heard from. One of the survivors, Owen Chase, the first mate of the *Essex,* wrote a narrative about the loss of the ship and the sufferings of the crew.

Equally terrible was the horrid mutiny on the whaleship *Globe* of Nantucket two years later. Samuel Comstock, a boat steerer, was the ringleader. The mutineers were armed with whaling implements, and the scuppers ran with blood. All the officers were murdered. Those who were not instantly killed were thrown overboard. Comstock took command, threatening to boil in the try-pots any man who disobeyed him. Eventually Comstock was himself killed by some of the crew who brought the murder ship safely into port. Two of the survivors, Lay and Hussey, wrote a narrative of the mutiny, and William Comstock wrote a life of his brother Samuel, the mutineer.

When the larger whaling ships came into use, Nantucket's supremacy as a whaling port was threatened be-

cause deep-draught vessels could not get over the bar outside Nantucket Harbor. Whalemen from Nantucket used
Edgartown Harbor at Martha's Vineyard to fit their ships
for sea and take on fresh water. Cargoes were sometimes
discharged there, too. It is said that from the lookout in
one of the Nantucket steeples overlooking the entire island, a watchman with a telescope could make out any
Nantucket vessel that came to anchor at Edgartown.

In the 1840's a large floating dry dock was used to get
large ships over the bar. It was called a camel. In the Old
State House Museum in Boston there is a painting of the
Zenas Coffin with 3,100 barrels of oil on board being
floated over the bar in the marine camel, which reduced
her draught from sixteen to eight feet. The *Coffin* is seen
passing the *Boston Packet* of not more than one hundred
tons which is aground. Edgartown, New Bedford, and
New London, with unobstructed harbors, had an advantage over Nantucket. New Bedford took the lead, but the
whaling industry as far as New England was concerned
was sinking fast. In a few years it had vanished altogether.

Many whalers were used to take gold seekers around
Cape Horn to California in 1849. During the Civil War
dozens of them were bought by the government to be sunk
in the channel approaches to southern harbors in an attempt to seal important Confederate ports. Old stone
walls in the vicinity of New Bedford supplied the cargoes
for these blockade ships.

A century ago the population of Nantucket was about
9,000, and some seventy ships were owned there, most of
them engaged in the whale fishery, with a considerable
fleet of smaller craft, chiefly schooners and sloops. When
Samuel Adams Drake, the historian, visited Nantucket
in 1875, the population had shrunk to a little more than

4,000, and today it is less than that. The industry which had won a reputation and riches for the island was gone by the time Drake got there. There was not a single whaler left. Yet less than twenty years before (1858), the *Watchman* of Nantucket had come home with a record take for one ship of eight hundred pounds of ambergris—the stuff that looks like suet but is worth hundreds of dollars a pound. A large proportion of the houses appeared to be unoccupied, though many which had long been vacant were being taken over for summer homes. Old brasses were being refurbished, and new brooms were sweeping the cobwebs away. The summer invasion, of course, destroyed much of the character and originality of old Nantucket, but it must have been a boon to many of the remaining islanders.

Perhaps the most outstanding reminders of the old whaling times to be seen today at Nantucket are the railed platforms atop the roofs of many old houses. These lookouts, called by some captain's walks and by others widow's walks, are a traditional feature of Nantucket building. Other New England seacoast places have adopted them to some extent, though in maritime Maine ship-owning families built cupolas on their houses for observatories instead of walks, perhaps because of Maine's severer climate. Retired Nantucket sea captains could take the air on their rooftop platforms, pacing up and down as on a deck, watching the arrival and departure of ships, and keeping an eye on the weather. Here women could scan the sea for tidings of their relatives. It is said that "formerly every other house in Nantucket had one of these lookouts, or a vane at the gable end to show if the wind was fair for vessels homeward-bound."

The town crier, whose modern counterpart is the radio

announcer, used to herald approaching ships with horn, bell, and voice. Nantucket retained its town crier longer, perhaps, than any place in New England. Some odd character was always available for the job, and, like the radio announcer, he had his paid commercial announcements to make. Billy Clark, who died in 1909, was town crier for forty years, and some folk thought he blew his fish horn so much that he literally blew his lungs away. Billy may have been the town crier about whom Samuel Adams Drake wrote the following amusing paragraph:

"This functionary I met, swelling with importance, but a trifle blown from the frequent sounding of his clarion, to wit, a japanned fishhorn. Met him, did I say? I beg the indulgence of the reader. Wherever I wandered in my rambles, he was sure to turn the corner just ahead of me, or to spring from the covert of some blind alley. He was one of those who, Macy says, knew all the other inhabitants of the island; me he knew for a stranger. He stopped short. First he wound a terrific blast of his horn. Toot, toot, toot, it echoed down the street, like the discordant braying of a donkey. This he followed with lusty ringing of a large dinner-bell, peal on peal, until I was ready to exclaim with the Moor,

> Silence that dreadful bell! it frights the isle
> From her propriety.

Then, placing the fish-horn under his arm, and taking the bell by the tongue, he delivered himself of his formula. I am not likely to forget it: 'Two boats a day! Burgess's meat auction this evening! Corned beef! Boston Theatre, positively last night this evening!'"

There is an interesting Indian legend concerning the fogs of Nantucket. It seems that a fabulous bird of ex-

traordinary size used to visit the south shore of Cape Cod
and carry away a great number of small children. Maushope, an Indian giant, who resided on the Cape, became
enraged at the depredations of the bird, and waded into
the sea in pursuit of it, till he had crossed the sound and
reached Nantucket. Before Maushope forded the sound
the Indians did not know the island existed. Maushope
found the children's bones under a large tree. Then de-
siring to smoke he ransacked the island for tobacco, but
finding none he filled his pipe with the usual Indian substitute for tobacco—poke weed. Ever since fogs have been
frequent at Nantucket and on the Cape. The Indians when
they saw the fog coming in would say, "There comes
Maushope's smoke."

There is another tradition that Nantucket was formed
by Maushope when he knocked out his pipe after smoking.

Nantucket is still a thriving fishing town. Despite the
loss of its greatest industry, the whale fishery, it has
weathered well the voyage into modern times.

Pirates

T HERE were pirates here once," said the man with the dolphin tattooed on his arm.

"My dear sir," said I, "there still are."

Visitors to the seacoast of New England soon discover that pirate legends and tales of buried treasure cling to it like barnacles. One of the most interesting legends tells of the trapping of a fugitive pirate in his den at Saugus, Massachusetts, during the Great Earthquake of 1658. Doubtless the pious and law-abiding folk of the time saw in the manner of the wretch's death a divine judgment on him for having followed watery pathways of iniquity. Earthquakes seem then to have had a chastening effect on New Englanders. Governor Hutchinson says that when terrestrial tremors caused a general apprehension of danger, destruction, and death, many people who had very little sense of religion appeared to be devout penitents. "But, too generally," he adds, "as the fears of another earthquake went off, the religious impressions went with them, and they returned to their former course of life."

In contrast to this, it is interesting to note that when New England was shaken by an earthquake in the early hours of December 20, 1940, a Saugus woman complained to the police by telephone, "There's a man on my porch who is shaking the windows and doors." Saugus, at the time of the trapping of the pirate, formed the west parish of Lynn. It was not until 1815 that it was made a separate town and given its present name, which was the Indian name of Lynn.

"One pleasant evening," says a local historian, "a little after sunset, a small vessel was seen to anchor near the mouth of Saugus River. A boat was presently lowered from her side, into which four men descended and moved up the river a considerable distance, when they landed, and proceeded directly into the woods. They had been noticed by only a few individuals; but in those early times, when the people were surrounded by danger, and easily susceptible to alarm, such an incident was well calculated to awaken suspicion, and in the course of the evening the intelligence was conveyed to many houses. In the morning, the people naturally directed their eyes toward the shore, in search of the strange vessel—but she was gone, and no trace could be found either of her or her singular crew. It was afterwards ascertained that, on that morning, one of the men at the iron works, on going into the foundry, discovered a paper, on which was written, that if a quantity of shackles, handcuffs, hatchets, and other articles of iron manufacture, were made and deposited, with secrecy, in a certain place in the woods, which was particularly designated, an amount of silver to their full value would be found in their place. The articles were made in a few days, and placed in conformity with the directions. On the next morning they were gone, and the money was found according to promise; but though a watch had been kept, no vessel was seen.

"Some months afterward," the narrative continues, "the four men returned, and selected one of the most secluded and romantic spots in the woods of Saugus for their abode. The place of their retreat was a deep narrow valley, shut in on two sides by high hills and craggy precipitous rocks, and shrouded on the others by thick pines, hemlocks, and cedars, between which there was only one small spot to which the rays of the sun at noon could penetrate. On climbing up the rude and almost perpendicular steps of the rock on the eastern side, the eye could command a full view of the bay on the south, and a prospect of a considerable portion of the surrounding country. The place of their retreat has ever since been called the Pirates' Glen, and they could not have selected a spot on the coast for many miles, more favorable for the purpose of concealment and observation. Even at this day, when the neighborhood has become thickly peopled, it is a lonely and desolate place, and probably not one in a hundred of the inhabitants has ever descended into its silent and gloomy recess. There the pirates built a small hut, made a garden, and dug a well, the appearance of which is still visible. It has been supposed that they buried money; but though people have dug there, and in several other places, none has ever been found. After residing there some time, their retreat became known, and one of the king's cruisers appeared on the coast. They were traced to their glen, and three of them were taken and carried to England, where it is probable they were executed. The other, whose name was Thomas Veal, escaped to a rock in the woods, about two miles to the north, in which was a spacious cavern, where the pirates had previously deposited some of their plunder. There the fugitive fixed his residence, and practised the trade of shoemaker, occasionally coming down to the village to obtain articles of sustenance. He continued his residence until the great earthquake this year, when the top of the rock was loosened, and crushed down into the mouth of the cavern, enclosing the unfortunate inmate in its unyielding prison. It has ever since been called the Pirate's Dungeon. A part of the cavern is still open, and is much visited by the curious."

Lawlessness seems to have first taken a marine form in New England about a dozen years after the Pilgrims landed at Plymouth, when Dixy Bull began preying on the English traders along the coast of Maine. Bull sacked Pemaquid and eluded the vessels which Governor Winthrop sent to take him. What became of him after that is not known, as he disappeared and was never seen again on the New England coast.

Maine became a popular pirate hangout, not because it offered rich opportunities for plunder, but because its lonely bays, coves, harbors, estuaries, and rivers afforded safe places for the high-seas robbers to careen and repair their ships. Machias Bay was a favorite haunt of two of these black-flag villains, John Rhoade and Samuel Bellamy. The latter ran into Machias River, got his ordnance ashore, and established batteries to protect his vessels while he had them hauled up for reconditioning. Bellamy was so taken with the place that he decided to return and make a stronghold of it, but before he was able to do this he was shipwrecked on Cape Cod, where he and most of his crew perished. The way in which this pirate met his end is told in the following excerpt from the *Collections of the Massachusetts Historical Society*:

"No shipwreck is more remarkable than that of the noted pirate Bellamy, mentioned by Governor Hutchinson, in his history. In the year 1717, his ship, with his whole fleet, were cast on the shore of what is now Wellfleet, being led near the shore by the captain of a snow, which was made a prize the day before, who had the promise of the snow as a present, if he would pilot the fleet into Cape Cod harbor; the captain suspecting the pirate would not keep his promise, and that, instead of clearing his ship, as was his pretence, his intention might be to plunder the inhabitants of Provincetown. The night being dark, a lantern was hung in the shrouds of the snow, the captain of which, instead of piloting where he was ordered, approached so near the land, that the pirates' large ship, which followed him, struck on the outer bar: the snow, being less, struck much nearer the shore. The fleet was put in confusion; a violent storm arose: and the whole fleet was shipwrecked on the shore. It is said that all in the large ship perished in the water except two. Many of the smaller vessels got safe on shore. Those that were executed, were the pirates put on board a prize schooner before the storm, as it is said. After the storm, more than an hundred dead bodies lay along the shore. At times, to this day [1793], there are king William and queen Mary's coppers picked up, and pieces of silver, called cob-money. The violence of the seas moves the sands upon the outer bar; so that at times the iron caboose of the ship, at low ebbs, had been seen."

Of course, so good a story as this luring of Bellamy to disaster and death called for a sequel, and the people of Cape Cod promptly obliged by supplying one with plenty of lively touches. The story is to be found in Alden's *Collection of Epitaphs,* where the author says:

"For many years after this shipwreck, a man, of a very singular and frightful aspect, used, every spring and autumn, to be seen travelling on the Cape, who was supposed to have been one of Bellamy's crew. The presumption is that he went to some place where money had been secreted by the pirates to get such a supply as his exigences required. When he died, many pieces of gold were found in a girdle, which he constantly wore. Aged people relate that this man frequently spent the night in private houses, and that, whenever the Bible or any religious book was read, or any family devotions performed, he invariably left the room. This is not improbable. It is also stated that, during the night, it would seem as if he had in his chamber a legion from the lower world; for much conversation was often overheard which was boisterous, profane, blasphemous, and quarrelsome in the extreme. This is the representation. The probability is, that his sleep was disturbed by a recollection of the murderous scenes in which he had been engaged, and that he, involuntarily, vented such exclamations as, with the aid of an imagination awake to wonders from the invisible regions, gave rise, in those days, to the current opinion that his bedchamber was the resort of infernals."

Thoreau was familiar with this tale of Bellamy and the sequel of the strange seafaring man who was thought to be one of his crew. He speaks of it in his Cape Cod book. He says the captain of the snow threw over a burning tar-barrel in the night, which drifted ashore, and the pirates followed it. He also relates an incident of his visit to the Cape which makes an interesting brief postscript to the pirate story.

"As I was walking on the beach in my visit," he says, "looking for shells and pebbles, just after that storm, which I have mentioned as moving the sand to a great depth, not knowing but I might find some cob-money, I did actually pick up a French crownpiece, worth about a dollar and six cents, near high water mark on the still moist sand, just under the abrupt, caving base of the bank. It was of a dark slate color, and looked like a flat pebble, but still bore a very distinct and handsome head of Louis XV., and the usual legend on the reverse, *Sit Nomen Domini Benedictum* (Blessed be the Name of the Lord), a pleasing sentiment to read in the sands of the sea-shore, whatever it might be stamped on, and I also made out the date, 1741."

The most notorious pirate ever to visit New England was Captain Kidd. He did not come to plunder, but rather to hide the plunder he had acquired on the Spanish Main and elsewhere. People with golden dreams still dig for the treasure which tradition says he buried somewhere along the coast. He was arrested in Boston and sent back to England. Upon his arrival there he was examined before the bar of the House of Commons, in an effort to pin part of the guilt for his piracies on the distinguished persons who had backed his expedition which had been to capture pirates and bring them to justice. Instead, he had taken to buccaneering on his own account.

Kidd made a poor showing at the bar of the House, for on his way to Parliament he visited other bars and turned up intoxicated. "This fellow!" exclaimed a member who had been most anxious to have Kidd examined. "I thought he had been only a knave, but unfortunately he happens to be a fool likewise."

Kidd was eventually tried in the courts and convicted. He suffered, with one of his companions, Darby Mullins, at Execution Dock on May 23, 1701. After Kidd had been tied up to the gallows the rope broke and he fell to the ground, but he was strung up again. He took advantage of the few further moments of life thus providentially allotted him to prepare his soul to meet its important change.

Pirates were executed between low and high watermark, or, to use the old phrase, "within the flux and reflux of the sea," because they were tried in the admiralty courts, and this strip of tide-washed territory was considered within the jurisdiction of the marine tribunals. The silver oar, the symbol of the admiralty courts, was carried before them to the place of execution, and their bodies were usually left hanging in chains on the gibbet or buried on the foreshore.

On Friday, July 19, 1723, there was a mass execution of pirates at Newport, the most extensive that ever took place at one time in the colonies, which drew people from all parts of New England. The bodies of the twenty-six pirates who were hanged at Gravelly Point were taken to the northern end of Goat Island and buried between low and high watermark. They were all young men.

Nearly twenty years before, in 1704, Captain Quelch and six other pirates were convicted and sentenced to death at Boston. "Sermons were preached in their hearing every day, and prayers made daily with them," according to a contemporary newspaper account. "And they were catechized and they had many occasional exhortations." Judge Sewall, who went to see the executions, said there were many people present, and the river was covered with boats filled with spectators.

"Mr. Cotton Mather," he wrote, "came with Captain Quelch & 6 others for execution from the Prison to Scarlett's Wharf and from thence in boat to the place of Execution. When the Scaffold was hoisted to a due height the seven Malefactors went up. Mr. Mather pray'd for them standing on the Boat. Ropes were all fastened to the Gallows save King who was Reprieved. When the Scaffold was let to sink there was such a Screech of the Women that my wife heard it sitting in our Entry next to the Orchard and was much surprised at it, yet the wind was sou-west. Our house is a full mile from the place."

The Mather method of administering the consolations of religion to doomed malefactors was to discourse at length on their wickedness and folly in this world and the horrible tortures which surely awaited them in the next. Ned Low, one of the worst of the eighteenth-century pirates, who hated New Englanders and once cut off the nose of a Yankee skipper just to "larn him to be a toad," probably had heard of the hanging sermons preached by Mather to condemned pirates. For after capturing and cruelly flogging some fisherman from the Isles of Shoals, he gave each his choice of cursing Parson Mather three times or being hanged. Every man Jack chose to curse the cleric.

The wholesale execution at Newport did not deter other pirates from cruising off the New England coast. Between August, 1723, and April, 1724, the noted pirate, John Phillips, took thirty-four vessels, plundering them of whatever he liked and killing or abusing the crews. In 1723 he took the fishing sloop *Dolphin* of Cape Ann and forced the able-bodied members of her crew to join him. One of the pressed fishermen was John Phillmore or Fillmore of Ipswich. The following April Phillips took the *Squirrel* of Annisquam, a fine new vessel on her maiden voyage, commanded by Captain Andrew Haraden. Phillips took a fancy to the *Squirrel* and abandoned his own vessel for her.

Three or four days afterward Captain Haraden with John Fillmore of the *Dolphin* and half a dozen other captives planned to retake the *Squirrel*. As the *Squirrel* was new and there was still some work to be done on her, the pirates had provided Haraden with the tools necessary to finish the job. At twelve o'clock, which it was agreed should be the zero hour, Captain Haraden being at work on deck and the sloop making good speed, Edward Cheeseman, one of the conspirators, suddenly seized the pirate master, John Nott, as he was walking on deck, and heaved him overboard. Haraden immediately killed Phillips with an adze, while another man attacked and slew the boatswain, Burrel, with a broadax. Others seized John Sparks, the pirate gunner, and threw him into the sea. The principal pirates thus being disposed of, the rest quickly surrendered.

Captain Haraden brought the *Squirrel,* with the head of Phillips at the masthead, into port. Four of the pirates were convicted, and two of them were hanged at Charlestown Ferry, June 2, 1724, after being well preached to by Dr. Sewall from Matthew xviii, 11. John Fillmore, who had been forced to serve as a pirate with Phillips, but who had assisted in the bloody business of retaking the *Squirrel,* was the great-grandfather of Millard Fillmore, thirteenth President of the United States.

Capture by pirates was generally followed by a period of uncertainty and suspense for the captive, during which he could only guess what fate was in store for him. Some pirate chiefs were amiable scoundrels, more like hosts than captors, while others were blackguards unspeakable, bent on making a terror of their names. Whether one fell into the hands of some affable Robin Hood of the waves, or some barbarous practitioner devoted to the realistic motto that dead men tell no tales, was a matter of luck. For the women captives the suspense must have been particularly harrowing.

The town of Marblehead, Massachusetts, has a legend of a screeching woman who was murdered by pirates in the seventeenth century. She was supposed to be the sole survivor of a captured merchantman, all the others on board having been slain when the ship was taken. To make the score perfect, the pirates brought her ashore one night near Oakum Bay and killed her. Her death screams were heard by the wives and children of some fishermen who lived in the vicinity, but in the absence of the men they

could do nothing for her. "Lord, save me! Mercy! O
Lord Jesus, save me!" cried the victim. They buried her
where she was murdered, and for many years, on the anniversary of the crime, her piercing screams were repeated.
Chief Justice Story, a native of Marblehead, averred that
he heard them again and again.

The old custom of executing pirates between high and
low watermark was not followed in New England after
the adoption of the Federal Constitution. The first person to be convicted and sentenced to death in the United
States Courts under the constitutional clause granting Congress the power "to define and punish piracies and fel-
onies committed on the high seas" was a seaman named
Thomas Bird, who was found guilty of piracy and murder
and hanged on Bramhall Hill at Portland, Maine, in 1790.
Portland was then called Falmouth, and Maine was still
part of Massachusetts.

In July, 1789, on returning from a fishing trip in his
schooner, *Betsy,* Captain Walter Jordan, when approaching Falmouth Harbor across Casco Bay, observed a
strange schooner apparently signaling for a pilot. There
was nothing unusual about this, and Captain Jordan approached and hailed the vessel, which he learned was the
Rover from Africa, Thomas Bird, master. Captain Jordan's offer to pilot the stranger into the harbor was accepted.

To the shrewd eyes of Captain Jordan, there seemed
to be something odd about the *Rover* from the first. There
was a crew of only three, Captain Bird, a Mr. Hansen,
and a Mr. Jackson, and although the vessel had, according to their story, come from Africa, she carried no cargo.
Nor did she seem to be looking for one. She made no
move to leave Falmouth and seemed to have no object in

coming there. Every day her crew went ashore to idle and
enjoy themselves in the sailor haunts along the waterfront.
This created some talk in Falmouth. As the vessel continued to stay in port, suspicion grew, and soon the whole
town was wondering why the *Rover* had come there.

If the crew had been a bit more circumspect, all this
local curiosity might have spent itself in idle chatter and
never have been brought to official attention at all. But
the three men had made friends with some of the sea-
going men of Falmouth, and some of these were invited
aboard the *Rover* of an evening to enjoy a game of cards
and a glass of grog. As the evening progressed, the sailors would grow merry and talkative and fall to swapping
yarns. Unfortunately for Bird and his crew, they told
conflicting stories concerning their voyage to Falmouth.

Captain Jordan's son, Robert Jordan, who was among
the *Rover's* guests, told authorities, "Sometimes they said
they had come right from England and hadn't been out
but twenty days when they arrived here. Sometimes they
said they'd been cruising on the coast of Africa to get a
load of niggers, but couldn't catch 'em. And then one of
'em says 'How many times do you think old Hodges has
looked over the ships news to try to find out our latitude
and longitude?'—and then he looked at the others and
winked and they all laughed.

"And one time it was a pretty dark evening, they had
drinked up all the liquor there was in the cabin, and Captain Bird told Hansen to get into the hold and bring up a
bottle of wine. Hansen kind of hesitated a little and
looked as if he didn't want to go, and said he didn't believe
but they'd had wine enough and he didn't want to go pok-
ing around in the hold at night. At that Captain Bird
called him a pretty baby and asked him what he was afraid

of, and wanted to know if he was afraid he should see
Connor there. And then Captain Bird ripped out a terrible
oath and swore he'd have some wine if the devil was in
the hold. And he went and got a bottle and give us all
another drink. When he came back again, Hansen asked
him if he see anything of Connor there. And Captain Bird
swore he'd throw the bottle of wine at his head if he didn't
shut up.

"Another time I was aboard in the daytime and I see
a parcel of red spots on the cabin floor and up along the
gangway that looked as if there'd been blood there and
I asked them what that was and they said it wasn't
nothin' only where they butchered a whale. And then they
all laughed again and looked at each other and winked."

William Dyer, another fisherman on the schooner *Betsy,*
reported that one day, when he was aboard the *Rover,* he
noticed a little round hole in a board in the after part of
the cabin that looked as if it might have been made by a
bullet from a gun, and that there were small holes spat-
tered around it that looked like shot holes. He took his
pen-knife and dug out a piece of shot from one of them.
When he inquired what they had been shooting there,
Hansen replied that that was where Captain Bird had
shot a porpoise when they were off the coast of Africa.
At this the crew exchanged meaning glances and laughed.

After full consideration of the various reports, the authorities ordered Stephen Hammond, a government officer, to arrest the crew of the *Rover.* Expecting a
struggle, he took eight men with him in a yawl and stood
at the helm while two rowed, and the other six stood with
their guns ready.

As Hammond and his men approached, they saw the

schooner begin to move in a light breeze down the harbor, evidently attempting to escape. But four of Hammond's men took to the oars and rowed so fast that they soon overhauled her. As they approached, they heard Bird call out, "H'ist the main sail, spring for your lives, and we'll beat them."

Between Cape Elizabeth and House Island the government men again caught up with the *Rover*. Hammond ordered Bird to heave to, but he kept on. Then Hammond shouted that if he didn't he'd shoot him as he stood at the helm. He ordered his men to take good aim and fire. At this, Bird leaped down the companionway, followed by the other two, and the schooner went adrift.

The government men brought the yawl alongside and boarded the *Rover*. On looking down into the cabin, they perceived that the three men were armed, Bird with a musket, and the others with a cutlass and handspike. Hammond quietly closed the companionway, and, as some of his men understood working a vessel, they soon beat up the harbor again and made fast to one of the wharves on the Falmouth side. The wharf was lined with people who had been watching the chase, and who now jumped aboard in crowds and thronged the vessel. The companionway was opened, and Bird and his men were ordered up. Perceiving that there were altogether too many guns for them to put up any resistance, they came up quietly and surrendered.

The three men were questioned in jail and ordered to identify themselves. The leader said his name was Thomas Bird, and that he was an Englishman. Hansen said he was a Swede, and Jackson that he was born in Newton, Massachusetts. The three had little confidence in each other.

Each thought that the others would betray him, and, reasoning that the one who made the earliest and fullest confession would be likely to receive the lightest punishment, they all confessed that the captain of the *Rover* had been killed on the voyage.

Their stories agreed on all important points. The vessel was owned by a certain Mr. Hodges in England, and her captain's name was Connor. The *Rover* had been trading for some time on the coast of Africa under Captain Connor, who was rough and arbitrary and abused his men beyond endurance.

One night, when they were all in the cabin, Captain Connor subjected them to his usual abusive and overbearing manner. Bird, who could contain himself no longer, caught up a loaded gun which stood in the cabin and shot Captain Connor dead on the spot. The crew then became exceedingly frightened and tried to dress his wounds and bring him to. As there were no signs of returning life, they took him on deck and threw him into the sea. They were afraid to return to England after what had happened. After consultation, they decided to come to the United States, dispose of such articles as they had on board, sell the vessel at the first opportunity, and then separate to return to their respective countries.

The case was tried before Judge John Lowell, who found Bird guilty, and the other two not guilty. Mr. Syms, who appeared for the defendants, moved in arrest of judgment, because the latitude and longitude of the sea where the crime was committed was not stated in the indictment. This was overruled, and the prisoner, Bird, was sentenced to death by the court.

Bird's counsel sent a petition for a reprieve or pardon

to the President of the United States, then residing in New York, but President Washington refused to interfere with the sentence of the court. The prisoner was hanged by Marshal Dearborn on Bramhall Hill on the last Friday of the month of June, 1790.

Cops and Robbers

THE million-dollar robbery of the National Bank of Northampton, Massachusetts, in 1876, was a terrible shock to the Yankee folk of that community. Many persons were ruined, while others who managed to weather the blow were for some time seriously embarrassed. The after effects of the looting were felt in Northampton for years.

The robbery was carefully planned and executed with hardly a hitch. In the early morning hours of Wednesday, January 26, 1876, five masked bandits entered the modest Elm Street home of John Whittelsey, the cashier of the Northampton National Bank. Two of them went directly to the bedroom of Mr. and Mrs. Whittelsey, and awakening them snapped handcuffs on their wrists. By the light of the japanned dark lantern which one of them carried, the Whittelseys saw that the masked intruders standing one on each side of their four-poster were equipped with revolvers. One of them, who appeared to be the leader and was addressed by the others as Number One, wore a long linen duster, such as travelers donned in those days when they went on railway journeys, while the other was clad in a short coat and overalls. Although muffled like assassins, neither used the rough speech of the underworld but spoke as if on a cultural level equal to or not far below that of their victims.

The other three robbers quickly rounded up the other inmates of the house and herded them into the Whittelseys' bedroom. Besides Mr. and Mrs. Whittelsey, there were five persons in the Elm Street dwelling that night. They were Mr. and Mrs. T. B. Cutler, a Miss Benton, a Miss White, and a servant girl, who was the most terrified one of the household. As soon as the robbers made certain that no one had been overlooked, they hustled these five captives off to other parts of the house, gagged them and bound them to the beds, and threatened them with violence if they stirred or tried to raise an alarm.

The leader then told Mr. Whittelsey to dress. Crossing the room to the closet to help him find his clothes, the robber seemed surprised at the meagerness of the banker's wardrobe.

"What, have you only one vest?" he exclaimed, and Mr. Whittelsey admitted that was all he owned.

When he had finished dressing, Mr. Whittelsey was told what his visitors had come for—the keys to the bank and the combination of the vault. They told him they knew definitely that he possessed these, and it would go hard with him if he didn't produce them immediately.

Mr. Whittelsey, who was a fattish, sandy, rather pompous little man, was no coward. "It's useless for you to try to break into the bank," he told them. "Its locks have been proven safe."

"We know more about locks than you do," said the man in the duster.

"I'll never betray my trust," added Mr. Whittelsey resolutely.

"We'll see about that," was the answer.

They took him downstairs where he was curtly told to hand over the bank keys. Mr. Whittelsey refused.

"Is this the key to the back door?" asked the bandit in overalls, fishing a key from the cashier's pocket.

"Yes," said Mr. Whittelsey.

"You lie," said the robber, fitting the key into the front door and turning the lock.

"Don't hit him yet," said the leader, as the other appeared on the point of striking the cashier. "He's ill." Then to Mr. Whittelsey, "Would you like some brandy?"

"No," replied the cashier, "I feel better now."

"Were you not at Watch Hill two years ago?" asked the linen-duster bandit.

"Yes, I was there," said Mr. Whittelsey.

"I was there too," said the cracksman, as if to impress his victim with the fact that he moved in the same social circles as bankers.

The next move showed how carefully the robbery had been planned down to the smallest detail. The leader took from his pocket a brand new pad of paper and a freshly-sharpened lead pencil, these articles having been provided expressly for the purpose of taking down the combination of the vault, which was now demanded of Mr. Whittelsey. He demurred at first, but finally gave some figures which were jotted down on the pad. He was then asked for the combination of the inner door.

"It isn't locked," said Mr. Whittelsey.

"That's a lie," said the leader, pointing his revolver at him.

Mr. Whittelsey gave a further series of figures, and was ordered to state the combination to the inside safe. As he hesitated, the robber jabbed him in the face with the sharp point of the pencil. Thus prodded, the cashier gave what purported to be the inside combination.

"Do you swear these figures are correct?" asked the leader, coming very close to him.

"Ye-es."

"Very well, let's hear you repeat them."

This Mr. Whittelsey could not do, so it was immediately plain the figures he had given were false.

"See, Number One, we're wasting our time," said the second in command. "We'll have to teach him to stop lying."

Whereupon the chief gave the cashier another vicious jab in the face with the pencil, shook him violently, and administered several stiff body blows that hurt.

"Will you tell us now?" he was asked.

There was no answer. Both robbers then went to work on him, beating him, kicking him, wringing his ears, throttling him, and brutally maltreating him after the fashion of police trying to extract information from a suspect. They held their revolvers to his head, threatening to shoot him if he didn't comply. They slammed him to the floor, and held a lighted candle to the soles of his feet.

For three hours they tried to break him with third-degree methods, but the little cashier held out against them. At length, along about four o'clock in the morning, when they had reduced him to a physical wreck, Mr. Whittelsey could bear it no longer and gave in to them. He produced the bank keys and gave the correct combinations to the vault.

Three of the robbers decamped immediately, leaving two of their number to guard the household. Mr. Whittelsey was taken upstairs, blindfolded, gagged, and lashed to his bed. One of the robbers who remained at the house improved the time by going through Mr. Whittelsey's clothes and taking fourteen dollars in cash and his gold watch and chain. At six o'clock, with only an hour of darkness left in which to make their escape, the two guards left the Whittelseys' home.

As soon as he was certain that the robbers had gone, John Whittelsey, bruised and aching from the hours of punishment he had undergone, began struggling to free himself from his bonds. An hour later he succeeded in getting loose and, after freeing the others, hastened to the bank. He reached the bank shortly after seven o'clock, to find the vault locked, the dials broken off. The extent of the loss, or whether there had actually been a robbery or not, it was impossible to say until a safe expert had opened the vault. The whole town was kept in suspense until late that night, when William Edson of Herring and Company of New York, manufacturers of safe equipment, got it open. It was found that the robbers had made a clean sweep. Over a million dollars' worth of cash and securities were missing.

Scholars on their way to the Bridge Street school in Northampton the morning after the robbery saw groups of men standing about near the bank and were quick to learn that the institution had been visited during the night by robbers. This in itself was thrilling news for the youngsters, but it was even more exciting when it was discovered afterward that for several weeks before the attack

on the bank the robbers had used the attic of the schoolhouse for a hiding place. As the children recited their lessons and did their school work, the bandits had been concealed in the same building. No one in Northampton
dreamed then or later that hidden under the teacher's platform and behind the blackboard in the Bridge Street
school was the treasure which had been stolen from the
bank.

The one inspiration the local police seem to have had
in the affair was that the thieves had cached the loot near
by and would return for it. This led to a search and the
discovery that the attic of the schoolhouse had been used
as a hideout. Here they found blankets, satchels, ropes,
moldy food, and a paper bag from the Stamford, Connecticut, restaurant of the New York, New Haven, and
Hartford Railroad. There was also a whiskey bottle bearing the label of a New York distributor, and a copy of
the New York *Sun* for December 22, 1875. A thorough
search of the schoolhouse by the police would have revealed the bank booty.

Patrols were established on all roads leading into town,
and a strict watch kept over all trains at the railroad station. These measures were continued for some time, but
it wasn't until after they had been relaxed that the robbers
drove into town one night with a pair of horses and removed the spoils.

At the Whittelsey home on Elm Street the robbers left
a miscellaneous collection of souvenirs, including masks,
dusters, rubbers, cords, straps, dark lanterns, a number of
sledge hammers, which apparently were used to break
open three doors of the house, and other tools. But none
of these things, nor the findings at the schoolhouse, gave
the authorities of Hampshire County any inkling as to

who had done the job. The bank offered a reward of $25,000 for the capture of the thieves and the return of the securities, but no one claimed it.

About a month after the robbery the bank received a letter from New York purporting to be from the robbers and seeking to negotiate with the bank for the return of the securities. The letter was printed in pen and ink and was unsigned. This is what it said:

"Dear Sirs,—When you are satisfied with detective skill, you can make a proposition to us, the holders, and if you are liberal, we may be able to do some business with you. If you entertain any such ideas, please insert a personal in the New York Herald. Address to XXX and sign 'Rufus,' to which due attention will be paid. To satisfy you that we hold papers, we send you a couple of pieces."

Enclosed with the letter were two stock certificates unmistakably the property of the bank. No attention was paid to this letter, which was followed by three more of similar character. In reply to one, however, the bank responded cautiously through an advertisement in the New York *Herald,* to which it received the following reply from New York, dated October 20, 1876.

"Gentlemen,—Since you have seen fit to recognize the receipt of our letter, we will send you our price for the return of the goods. The U. S. coupon bonds and money taken cannot be returned; but everything else—bonds, letters, and papers, to the smallest document, will be returned for 150,000 dollars. If these figures suit you, we will make arrangements according to our promise, and you may have the goods as soon as preliminaries can be arranged for the safe conduct of business. If you agree to this price, insert in the New York Herald personal column the simple word, 'Agatha.'

> "Respectfully,
> "Rufus."

By this time it was apparent that the Northampton National Bank had been robbed by an extremely clever gang of crooks. It was also clear that the local police after months of work were no nearer a solution than they had been the morning after the robbery. The bank officials, activated perhaps by the impatience of the depositors, at last decided to call in the Pinkertons. This famous detective agency possessed more information about crime and criminals than any other organization in the country. It was familiar with the methods used by bank robbers. Certain aspects of the Northampton bank case which meant nothing to the local police were full of meaning for the Pinkertons.

It should be recalled that after the Civil War bankers who had worried about the security of their vaults began to lose less sleep, thanks to the inventions of Linus Yale, the locksmith. Linus, who was a descendant of the Yale family of New Haven, was born in New York State in 1821. He began life as a portrait painter, but the strong mechanical bent he possessed soon asserted itself, and he turned his hand to lock making. He established his first shop at Shelburne Falls, Massachusetts, on the Deerfield River, about twenty-five miles from Northampton. Locksmiths were then really smiths who made locks by hand. Linus was particularly interested in bank locks, perhaps because they brought the highest prices. At any rate, during the eighteen-fifties he built up quite a reputation for himself with his Yale Infallible Bank Lock, his Yale Magic Bank Lock, and his Yale Double Treasury Bank Lock—names suggesting that Linus had a flair for marketing locks as well as inventing them. But it was during the Civil War that he made his greatest contributions as a locksmith. In 1862 he produced the first combination, or dial, lock, which he called the Monitor Bank Lock, following this in 1863 with the Yale Double Dial Bank Lock, in the construction of which he established principles since largely followed. During this same period he also invented the lock for which he is best known—the cylinder lock with the flat key, the idea for which he took from the ancient Egyptians. Linus Yale died in 1868, but by that time it looked as if Yale locks and the improvements made by the safe manufacturers in strengthening vaults had at last made banks burglar proof.

In 1872, however, there began a wave of bank robberies, culminating in the great Northampton robbery, which caused uneasiness among bankers throughout the country. These robberies were carefully organized and carried out with daring and skill. Despite the new locks and vaults, no bank seemed to be safe against the depredations of these burglars. The Pinkertons had been called in on a number of these cases, but thus far had been unable to trace a single robbery to the gang they suspected. Because of certain resemblances which the robberies bore to each other the Pinkertons were convinced that the same band was responsible for all. It was the practice of this gang, for example, after a robbery to bargain for the return of the stolen securities in one lot, instead of dividing them and letting each member negotiate for himself, as was the custom among most bands of bank robbers. Thus, the letters written to the Northampton bank had a special significance for the Pinkertons.

Although they had not been able to pin anything on them,

the Pinkertons were convinced that two New York sporting men, Robert Scott and James Dunlap, were the brains of a criminal organization specializing in bank robberies. Scott had a prison record, having served two terms in the Illinois Penitentiary, one for grand larceny, the other for assault. During his second term he became acquainted with a veteran bank robber, one Thomas Riles, alias Scarfaced Tom, through whom, following their release from prison, he met James Dunlap, a young Scotchman. Scott and Dunlap were men of the same stamp and got along very well together. Both had expensive tastes, both were cool, daring, clever, and seemingly always in the pink of condition in spite of the wild life they led. And both thought, ate, drank, breathed, and dreamed bank business. Following a robbery they did not go into hiding, but were to be seen as usual about their customary haunts. There was, indeed, much surprise in sporting circles when the popular pair were finally unmasked.

The Pinkertons with their accustomed thoroughness checked up on all persons intimately associated with the bank, including those who had served it in any way, and it was while investigating these people that the Pinkertons picked up a lead that eventually enabled them to get Scott and Dunlap. It will be recalled that the expert who opened the safe after it was pillaged was William Edson, an employee of Herring and Company. He was in Bristol, Connecticut, the day after the robbery, and as soon as the safe company in New York received word from the Northampton bank that the locks of the vault had been wrecked, a telegram was sent to Edson to proceed at once to Northampton. There was nothing extraordinary in this, but Robert Pinkerton was a man with a good memory, a picker up of unconsidered trifles, with which he often worked wonders. And Pinkerton soon began to take a deep interest in William Edson.

A couple of months before the robbery Edson had carefully inspected the lock and dials of the Northampton vault. After the robbery he had gone out of his way to urge the officials of the bank to bargain with the robbers for the return of the stolen securities, offering to act as go-between and even going so far as to state to one of the directors that he knew by name the men who had committed the robbery. When questioned by the Pinkertons, Edson admitted trying to persuade the directors to negotiate with the robbers, but denied having done so for any other reason than his sympathy for the ruined depositors of the bank.

Repeated reports had reached Robert Pinkerton that the gang responsible for the recent series of bank lootings had for a confederate an expert in locks and safes who tipped them off to the most vulnerable banks and gave them invaluable technical advice on how these institutions could be tapped. But this was only a rumor. No particular person had been indicated, except that he was said to be a man of undoubted skill and spotless reputation. Then suddenly Robert Pinkerton recalled a trifling incident connected with another bank robbery.

The previous autumn Pinkerton had been called into the case of the robbery of the First National Bank of Pittston, Pennsylvania, a job which had netted the thieves some $60,000. As was quite usual in those days, the representatives of the various safe manufacturers, among whom competition was keen, had flocked to the scene of the robbery, in the hope of selling the bank new safety equipment. Pinkerton and some of these safe salesmen were examining the ruined vault, stepping over the litter caused by the explosion, when one of them picked up an air pump abandoned by the cracksmen.

"I could have sworn that this pump belonged to my company," said the salesman, examining it closely, "but that, of course, is impossible."

He went on to explain that the pump was identical with a special one that had been designed by his company for demonstration purposes. Pinkerton remembered that this salesman worked for Herring and Company.

Weeks and months passed as the Pinkertons worked unremittingly to build up a case against the Scott and Dunlap gang. They still lacked sufficient evidence to convict any of the suspects, but they felt the time was ripe to see what could be done with Edson, who had been kept under constant surveillance. Accordingly, George Bangs, one of the best men in the Pinkerton Agency, was assigned the task of extracting a confession from Edson. Bangs told Edson bluntly that the Pinkertons knew the Scott and Dunlap gang had robbed the Northampton bank and that he was an accomplice. Bangs said further the gang had been trailed for weeks and the detectives might close in at any time. Once they were apprehended, the robbers would try to save themselves by turning against Edson. None of the pack would hesitate a minute to sacrifice him. Bangs was a cool, convincing talker, and when he wound up by flatly giving Edson his choice of a twenty-year prison sentence for bank robbery or his freedom and a generous money award for confessing his part in the robbery, Edson broke down and elected to tell all. When he had finished there wasn't much the Pinkertons did not know about the Scott and Dunlap gang and the Northampton robbery.

In telling how he happened to fall among thieves, Edson explained that before the Civil War he had been a prosperous New England merchant, a man of means and of good repute in the city where he carried on his business. Like many New Englanders, Edson sold quantities of merchandise in the Southern states largely on credit, and the outbreak of the Civil War wiped him out completely. He then took a position as a safe salesman with Herring and Company and moved to New York. Although he did well in his new work, he had a weakness for fast horses, spending far more than he could afford, with the result that he ran heavily into debt.

By chance Edson kept one of his horses in a livery stable operated by a man named Ryan, a shady character, who was connected with the Scott and Dunlap gang. Ryan was friendly to Edson, and when the latter could no longer pay for the stabling of his horse and talked with Ryan about selling the animal, the liveryman saw an opportunity to sound Edson out about the possibility of his helping Scott and Dunlap with his confidential knowledge of banks and locks.

"If I had your position," said Ryan, "I'd never lack for money."

"I don't know what you mean," said Edson.

"Oh," said Ryan, "there are plenty of people who would pay well to learn some of the things you know about safes and banks."

The suggestion made Edson indignant, and nothing more was said at the time, but occasionally Ryan reverted to it.

Time passed and Edson's financial position grew steadily worse. Finally, he brought up the subject himself.

"What is it these people want to know?" Edson asked Ryan.

"Well," said Ryan, who knew of a special problem then facing the gang, "they would like to know, for one thing, if there is any way of beating these new Yale locks."

"You can't pick a Yale lock," said Edson. "That would take too long. But there's a way of getting one open."

"How?" asked Ryan.

"Oh, we'll talk that over some day," said Edson and walked away.

The Yale lock that was giving the Scott and Dunlap gang trouble was in the door of the Y.M.C.A. at Elmira, New York. There was nothing in the Y.M.C.A. which the gang wanted, but the rooms of the association were over the Second National Bank, a federal depository, and directly beneath one of the rooms was the bank vault, containing two hundred thousand dollars in cash and six millions in bonds. It was this treasure the robbers were after. It would have been an easy matter to break into the Y.M.C.A., but the plan was to get at the vault by digging down through the heavy masonry above it, and this meant nightly visits to the Y.M.C.A., perhaps for weeks. To smash the lock would have excited suspicion. An attempt was made to get an impression of the key by borrowing the secretary's without his knowledge, but when the thieves broke into his house one night and searched his clothes they couldn't find it, as the secretary had hidden the key under a piece of carpeting.

Scott and Dunlap sent a member of the gang named Perry to New York to learn how to open the lock. Ryan introduced Perry to Edson, who was now willing to talk with the crooks, and Perry persuaded him that he could make a fortune with perfect safety simply by giving the gang confidential information about banks and safes. He offered Edson a fifty-thousand-dollar share in the robbery of the Elmira bank if he would tell them how to open the Y.M.C.A. lock. Edson accepted Perry's proposal and agreed to go to Elmira.

To justify Edson's trip to Elmira, Scott and Dunlap sent an inquiry about safes to Herring and Company, and Edson was sent there in answer to the lead, to see if he could make a sale. At Elmira he saw Scott, and told him to put the lock out of commission that night by sliding a delicate sliver of wood into it. Meanwhile, Edson would let the bank know he was in town, with the idea that he would be sent for to fix the lock when it was found to be out of order the next morning. This would enable him to take an impression of the key. Edson's little scheme worked, and the gang was soon engaged in the work of digging through the masonry to the vault.

Weeks of hard labor went into the job. Each night they took up the carpet and floor boards in the Y.M.C.A. above the vault and chipped away at the masonry, carrying the debris in baskets to the top of the opera house adjoining the bank. Literally tons of material were removed. When they finally got down to the vault itself a trivial mishap wrecked their plans. Powdery, white dust settling on the floor of the vault aroused suspicion. The investigation that followed disclosed what had been going on and the gang fled. Perry, however, was caught and got five years in Auburn, but the robbers were playing for big stakes, and this was one of the hazards of the game.

It was discovered afterward that while in Elmira the gang lived in a house which was rented and furnished by a woman who kept house for them. She told people her husband was a traveling salesman who came home infrequently, and as the gang only left the house at night, slipping out one at a time, the curiosity of the neighbors was not aroused. This same woman did the same thing for the gang in other places where they worked.

Better fortune rewarded the Scott and Dunlap gang in their next venture, which was an attack on a bank in Quincy, Illinois. Again they dug down from above and this time succeeded in getting into the vault and blowing the inside safe by a new method taught them by Edson. This was to seal the seams of the safe doors with putty or soap, except for two small holes at the top and bottom. Then as gunpowder was poured in at the top hole an air pump operated at the bottom one drove the powder into all the crevices around the doors. The charge was set off by a small pistol firing a blank cartridge and discharged by means of a string. Edson on his visits to banks used to demonstrate with a pump how easy it would be to blow open a safe, and would then try to sell a special padding put out by Herring and Company to prevent the air pump method from being successfully used. In the Quincy robbery the Scott and Dunlap gang got one hundred and twenty thousand in cash and approximately seven hundred thousand dollars in bonds which they sold back to the bank.

This haul was almost as rich as the gang's first big robbery in 1872, when two hundred thousand dollars was taken from a Louisville bank. The only person disappointed in the Quincy affair was Edson, who was paid only a small part of what he had been promised for the use of the air pump. He was bitter at the way Scott and Dunlap threw money away in high living in New York. Scott even bought a famous trotter, Knox, with whom he cut a great figure as a gentleman driver at the Coney Island course. But for every successful robbery the gang had its failures and narrow escapes from capture. In several instances they had their hands practically on the money but could not tarry long enough to get it.

By threats and promises Edson was won over once more. Several unsuccessful attempts were made against banks in New England and elsewhere, and then came the robbery of the Pennsylvania bank, where the tell-tale pump that put Robert Pinkerton on Edson's trail was left.

In the summer of 1875, after Scott and Dunlap had promised to make Edson an equal partner in the division of the spoils of the gang's robberies, Edson visited North-ampton under pretext of doing business for Herring and Company but in reality to explore the possibilities of loot-ing one of the banks there. As a result of this trip, they originally planned to rob the First National Bank, but at the last moment the scheme was abandoned, owing to a letter received by Herring and Company from the bank, in which it was stated that the bank had no faith in its locks and intended to change them for new ones. It was Edson's belief, shared by Scott and Dunlap, that inasmuch as the bank was alarmed about the security of its vault, ex-tra precautions would be taken to guard it which would make any attempt to rob the place unduly hazardous.

Edson then turned his attention to the Northampton National Bank. In November he inspected the vault, and at his suggestion the combination was entrusted to Mr. Whittelsey rather than to one of the younger members of the bank staff. On his return to New York, Edson was able to give Scott and Dunlap a detailed picture of the situ-ation, including the location of the cashier's house, the number of persons in the household, and much other in-formation. While using the Bridge Street school for a hideout, the gang spent weeks familiarizing themselves with the ground and planning everything down to the final escape. There were no automobiles in those days, and the getaway was apt to present difficulties.

Looking back it seems possible that no one would have been brought to justice for the great Northampton bank robbery had it not been for the blunder Scott and Dunlap made in trying to cheat Edson of his share of the spoils. While encouraging him in his efforts to bargain with the bank, they were themselves trying to effect a settlement behind his back, with every intention of freezing him out. It began to dawn on Edson that there was no truth in the adage about there being honor among thieves, at least, as far as Scott and Dunlap were concerned. It was almost a year after the robbery when matters finally came to a showdown. Edson had a meeting with the two leaders and Red Leary. A fierce quarrel ensued during which the gangsters threatened to murder Edson. He then determined to get them and extricate himself by freely confessing his part in the crime.

After Edson had confessed to Bangs, the Pinkertons moved quickly to get the ringleaders. On St. Valentine's Day, 1877, Scott and Dunlap were arrested in Philadelphia as they were on the point of entraining for the South bent on robbing another bank. No time was lost in taking them to Massachusetts, where they were arraigned and held for trial.

The case came up in July, 1877. As it was feared an attempt might be made to rescue the prisoners, Northampton citizens volunteered for extra guard duty at the jail. People who saw Scott and Dunlap tried were impressed by the superior appearance of the pair; they did not look like criminals. One incident of the trial that seems to have impressed the local ladies present was a gesture made one day by Scott. As he was being led out after a session of the court, he reached quickly over and picked up with his free hand a photograph of his wife lying on one of the tables and, holding it between his teeth, tore the picture in two and flung the pieces back. Scott and Dunlap were convicted largely on the evidence of the two New Englanders, John Whittelsey, who definitely identified them, and William Edson, who related his story as a witness for the Commonwealth of Massachusetts. Scott and Dunlap both received twenty-year sentences.

Several matters still remained to be cleared up, the most important of which was the recovery of the seven hundred thousand dollars' worth of securities. Edson had told Bangs that the only person who knew where they were was Dunlap. The Pinkertons figured that as soon as Dunlap was arrested he would have to share the secret with some other member of the gang, and not long after they learned that Scott's wife had passed the information along to Red Leary.

Red Leary was the most colorful member of the Scott and Dunlap gang. He was a notorious New York thug, a huge, red-haired, ugly-looking man, weighing close to three hundred pounds and as strong as a bull. He wore an eight and a quarter size hat which he claimed was bigger than that worn by any contemporary American statesman. He had nearly lost his eyesight while blowing a safe, and declared that but for this handicap he could lick John L. Sullivan and Paddy Ryan. He had an excellent record as a bold and fearless fighter in the Civil War.

Robert Pinkerton arrested Leary in New York, but while Leary was awaiting extradition he escaped from the Ludlow Street jail and fled to Europe. He soon returned, however, and was captured by Pinkerton and three of his men while sleighing in Brooklyn. They lost no time in taking him to Northampton.

Scott and Dunlap, hoping perhaps for some mitigation of their sentences, wrote to Leary from prison, saying they would not testify against him if he would surrender the securities to the bank, and this Leary did. During the two years the securities were held by the gang they depreciated in value one hundred thousand dollars. The cash and the bonds were never recovered.

Scott and Dunlap were the only ones to go to prison for the Northampton bank robbery. Leary and two other members of the gang were released because of insufficient evidence. But the capture and conviction of the leaders brought about a speedy liquidation of the gang. Scott died in prison after serving only a few years of his sentence. Dunlap, after serving a large portion of his, was pardoned. What became of him is not known. Red Leary was killed in New York some ten years after the robbery by being hit in the head with a brick. He and some of his cronies were coming out of a saloon one night when one of the party in a sportive mood picked up a brick and, throwing it up in the air, cried, "Look out for your heads, boys!" The joke proved fatal for Leary, whose skull was fractured by the falling brick.

The Northampton National Bank is still doing business, but in a new building, not the one occupied at the time of the robbery. Nor is John Whittelsey's house standing. It was bought and used for some time by Smith College, but a number of years ago was torn down to make way for a new dormitory. When recently I asked a resident of Northampton, who remembers John Whittelsey, if he was blamed for divulging the combination of the bank vault the answer was, "Oh, no. He had everybody's sympathy."

The Condemned

THE quaint old New England custom of hanging by
proxy, or executing an innocent old man in place
of some guilty young fellow whose services in the
work of colonization and deforestation could not be
spared, is one of those ludicrous fables without any fac-
tual foundation which has nevertheless found believers.
The story was a great favorite with Governor Dudley of
Massachusetts, who used to tell the following version of it
with gusto:

"One day, while a carpenter was cutting down a tree,
and a crowd of Indians stood around, watching every blow
with the greatest attention, the tree fell upon one of them
who did not get out of the way, killing him on the spot.
The other Indians set up a great howling over the dead
body, while the frightened carpenter ran and hid himself
to escape their vengeance; for they foolishly thought him
to blame for the death of their companion. The English
tried to persuade them that the carpenter was not at fault;

but nothing short of his death would pacify them. They demanded that he should be given up to them for execution. Seeing them thus enraged, and fearing that they might fall upon and destroy them, the English finally promised to hang the unlucky carpenter themselves.

"The Indians were told to come the next morning, and they would see him hanging from a particular tree. But the carpenter being a young and lusty fellow, and very useful, they concluded that they could not spare him; and there being in the fort an old bedridden weaver who had not long to live, he was taken out to the tree and quietly hanged in the room of the carpenter, to the entire satisfaction of the Indians, who did not detect the cheat, and who became good friends again."

The story seems to have originated with Thomas Morton, the scapegrace lawyer of Merry Mount, whom the Puritans banished from New England. He was the first to mention it in his *New England Canaan,* published in 1632. He said that after the settlement of Weston's colony at Weymouth, Massachusetts, one of the adventurers stole a capful of corn from an Indian granary which he accidentally discovered in the forest. The Indian owner, finding by the footprint that the thief was an Englishman, came and made his complaint at the plantation. The chief commander of the company called together a "parliament" of the people, "to pass upon this huge complaint, that a knife or string of beads would well enough have disposed of," and it was decided that the offense "was felony, and by the laws of England, punished with death; and this must be put in execution, for an example, and to appease the savage."

Straightway a man arose and said he had an idea that would aptly serve to satisfy the savages' complaint and at the same time would save the life of the young and lusty thief, who could ill be spared. This oration was well received by everyone, and the orator was entreated to tell how this end might be reached.

"You all agree that one must die," he said, "and one shall die. This young man's clothes we will take off, and put on one that is old and impotent, a sickly person that cannot escape death. Such is the disease on him confirmed, that die he must. Put the young man's clothes on this man, and let the sick person be hanged in the other's stead."

"Amen!" cried his hearers.

Morton then goes on to say that this would most likely have proved their final sentence had not one of them with a ravenous voice begun to croak and bellow, alleging that such a deceit if found out would exasperate the savages, and that the whites must show their zeal for justice by hanging the real offender. And this was the verdict reached, but they were uncertain how to carry it out, as the condemned was a dangerous man. "He was a person that in wrath did seem a second Samson, able to beat out their brains with the jawbone of an ass." One must admire the way in which they did it. "They called the man, and by persuasion got him fast bound in jest, and then hanged him up hard by in good earnest."

Morton, it will be observed, who was amused by the suggestion put forward at the meeting, is careful to state that they hung the actual thief and not a substitute. Yet Morton's tale is undoubtedly the basis of the one told by Samuel Butler in *Hudibras,* in which he has the New Englanders hang an old bedridden weaver instead of the real culprit, as in Governor Dudley's version. Butler alleged in a note to his poem that the story was true, but he was mistaken. Hanging by proxy is just an old fable with a vinous quality that has not deteriorated with age.

Many crimes were punishable by death in the colonial era. By the original laws of Massachusetts Bay eleven offenses were made capital. These were idolatry, witchcraft, blasphemy, murder, bestiality, sodomy, adultery, rape, man stealing, false witness, and conspiracy. In 1646 two additions of a startling character were made to the laws of 1642. "Any child above sixteen who shall curse or smite their [*sic*] natural father or mother shall be put to death, unless it can be shown that the parents have been unchristianly negligent in their education, or so provoked them by extreme and cruel correction that they have been forced to preserve themselves from maiming and death. Any son, above sixteen years, stubborn and rebellious, who will not obey his father or mother, and when they have chastened him will not hearken to them, they may take him before the court, and on their testimony that he is stubborn and rebellious and lives in sundry notorious crimes, such a son shall be put to death."

To these were added, in 1692, high treason, concealing the death of a bastard child, arson, and piracy, a total of seventeen offenses. Yet the number of capital offenses was at no time so great as in England.

Executions were public and drew multitudes of people. Modern opinion is against such exhibitions, but from the point of view of the condemned something can be said for dying in the open air before a crowd. It must have fortified many a poor wretch for the ordeal, enabling him to draw on the last reserves of his vanity. It probably also helped him to bear up during the delivery of the sermon customarily preached before a felon was launched into the fourth dimension. These hanging sermons were some-

times fearfully long. In a case at Taunton, Massachusetts,
in which a black boy murdered his mistress with a flatiron,
not one but several lengthy sermons were preached during
the prisoner's last days. The clergy, apparently scenting an
unusual opportunity to drive home the moral that crime
does not pay, clustered like flies in the shadow of the scaffold.

One of the most ghastly executions ever carried out
in New England took place at Redding, Connecticut, when
a Tory spy and a deserter from the American army were
executed on what is known to this day as Gallows Hill.
General Putnam, who was in command of the Continental
troops in winter quarters at Redding, had been so troubled
by desertions from his ranks and the activities of Tory
spies in the territory covered by his patrols that he resolved to make an example of the next offenders who
should fall into his hands. Perhaps he cannot be blamed,
however, for the fact that the executions which followed
were badly bungled.

From the papers of Lieutenant Samuel Richards, pay-
master in Colonel Wyllys's Connecticut regiment, we learn
that on February 4, 1779, "was tried at General Court
Martial Edward Jones for going to and serving the enemy,
and coming out as a spy—found guilty on each and every
charge Exhibited against him, and according to the law
and Usages of nations was sentenced to suffer death." We
are further told, "The General approves the sentence to
be put into Execution between the hours of ten and eleven
A.M. by hanging him by the neck till he be dead."

From the same source we learn that two days later a
second man was condemned to die. "At the Gen'l Court
Martial was tried John Smith of the 1st Connecticut Regiment for desertion and attempting to go to the Enemy,

found guilty, and further persisting in saying that he will go to the Enemy if ever he has an opportunity, Sentenced to be shot to death and orders that it be put in Execution between the hours of ten and twelve A.M."

Putnam decided to make a double job of it and execute the two men on the same day in as impressive a manner as possible. The following account of the execution is from Barber's *Connecticut Historical Collections*. Barber states that he derived the particulars from an aged inhabitant of Redding, who was present on the occasion and stood but a few feet from Jones when he was hanged.

"The scene which took place at the execution of these men is described as shocking and bloody. The man on whom the duty of hangman devolved, left the camp, and on the day of execution could not be found. A couple of boys about the age of twelve years, were ordered by Gen. Putnam to perform the duties of the absconding hangman. The gallows was about twenty feet from the ground. Jones was compelled to ascend the ladder, and the rope around his neck was attached to the cross beam. General Putnam then ordered Jones to jump from the ladder.

" 'No, General Putnam,' said Jones, 'I am innocent of the crime laid to my charge; I shall not do it.'

"Putnam then ordered the boys before mentioned to turn the ladder over. These boys were deeply affected with the trying scene; they cried and sobbed loudly, and earnestly entreated to be excused from doing any thing on this distressing occasion. Putnam drawing his sword ordered them forward, and compelled them at the sword's point to obey his orders.

"The soldier that was shot for desertion, was but a youth of 16 or 17 years of age. Three balls were shot through his breast; he fell on his face, but immediately turned over on his back; a soldier then advanced, and putting the muzzle of his gun near the convulsive body of the youth, discharged its contents into his forehead. The body was then taken up and put into a coffin; the soldiers had fired their pieces so near that they set the boy's clothes on fire, which continued burning. An officer with a drawn sword stood by while every soldier of the three brigades who were out on the occasion, was ordered to march by and look at the mangled remains. The bones of this young man were dug up a few years since for anatomical purposes. They were known to be his from the fracture of the skull; the bones, however, were of little or no use, for on exposure to the air they soon fell to pieces."

Following the publication of this account by Barber, attempts were made to discredit it. Other and less grim versions of the affair were presented by other historians; but Charles Burr Todd, author of the *History of Redding* (1880), who took particular care to investigate the matter thoroughly, says the weight of the evidence favors Barber. The two boys forced by Putnam to throw the spy from the ladder add, of course, the crowning touch of horror. Like the two children in Henry James's ghost story, they give an extra turn of the screw to the gruesome effect. This was too much even for Mr. Todd, who doubted that part of the story, but the boys do not seem like an invention. The person who arouses curiosity is the absconding hangman. Why had he no heart for the job? To this question there seems to be no answer. As for Old Put, as he was affectionately called, one remembers his pithy answer to Governor Tryon's letter demanding the restoration of a Tory lieutenant whom Putnam had captured. "Sir,—Nathan Palmer, a lieutenant in your king's service, was taken in my camp as a spy; he was tried as a spy; he was condemned as a spy; and he shall be hanged as a spy.—P.S. Afternoon. He is hanged."

There are no blacker pages in New England history than those dealing with the witchcraft trials and executions, which reached a climax at Salem in 1692. Witches taken in their alleged mischief were abominably visited by the law. Many were executed on evidence insufficient to have hanged a cat. The confessions of some show plainly that they were made by eccentric or mad old women. No sane person would have confessed, as one of the witches did, that she had had intercourse with the devil and looked forward to meeting him again. Doubtless some of the accused could have escaped the gallows by confessing to a bit of witchcraft, but they preferred to die rather than tell an untruth. It was an age when men and women could for a principle go to their deaths as to a feast.

The worst aspect of the business was the part played by children, who in some cases even accused their own parents. These juvenile delinquents succeeded in doing a lot of mischief. One unpleasant little creature, who started to denounce a respectable couple for putting their necromancy on her, was turned on so sharply that she admitted there was no truth in what she said. Asked why she did it, her answer was, "Just for fun." These children, who gave their evidence simply and calmly and followed it with spasms, managed to send about a score of persons to the gallows.

No figure stands out so magnificently during the Salem troubles as the eighty-year-old Giles Corey, who, because he sat silent before his judges when charged with witchcraft and refused to plead, incurred the awful penalty of *peine forte et dure,* which, in simple English, is the prolonged agony of being slowly pressed to death under massive weights. Longfellow made the indomitable old man the hero of one of his *New England Tragedies*, but there is an anonymous ballad, composed in the old style, which tells the story briefly and effectively.

Giles Corey was a Wizard strong,
    A stubborn wretch was he;
And fitt was he to hang on high
    Upon the Locust-tree.

So when before the magistrates
    For triall he did come,
He would no true confession make,
    But was compleatlie dumbe.

"Giles Corey," said the Magistrate,
    "What has thou heare to pleade
To these that now accuse thy soule
    Of crimes and horrid deed?"

Giles Corey, he said not a worde,
    No single word spoke he.
"Giles Corey," said the Magistrate,
    "We'll press it out of thee."

They got them then a heavy beam,
    They laid it on his breast;
They loaded it with heavy stones,
    And hard upon him prest.

"More weight!" now said this wretched man;
    "More weight!" again he cried;
And he did no confession make,
    But wickedly he dyed.

Under English law the reason why one charged with crime would refuse to plead was that if he did plead and was found guilty his property was forfeited to the crown. On the other hand, if he did not plead and was found guilty he incurred the fearful penalty of *peine forte et dure,* but his property was saved to his heirs. Many men in England endured the terrible ordeal of pressing for the sake of their families. Whether this or some other reason was the cause of Giles Corey's silence, I do not know. His case was the only one of its kind in New England.

The variety of punishments which could be meted out by the courts to offenders against the criminal laws was much greater in colonial times and during the early years of the republic than it is now. Besides being fined and imprisoned, a man might be whipped, branded, caged, have his ears cropped, be made to sit in the stocks, stand in the pillory, or ride the wooden horse. As a probationary measure, he was sometimes compelled to wear a halter around his neck whenever he appeared in public. If caught without it, he was scourged. Persons whose ears had been cropped sometimes let their hair grow to hide the fact.

Riding the wooden horse was a punishment to which horse thieves were sometimes sentenced. In 1785 Moses Parker was convicted at Hartford of horse stealing and sentenced "to sit on a wooden horse half an hour, receive fifteen stripes, pay a fine of £10, be confined in gaol and the work house three months, and every Monday morning for the first month to receive ten stripes and sit on the wooden horse aforesaid." To judge from newspaper reports, riding the wooden horse was not much of an ordeal for the rider.

"The Supreme Court, at their present session," says

the Connecticut *Courant,* "has tried and convicted several persons, of the crimes of forgery, horse stealing, and the villains received their respective punishments. One of the rogues was sentenced to ride the wooden horse, that wonderful refinement of punishment in our modern statutes. Accordingly on Thursday last, the terrible machine was prepared—consisting of one simple stick of wood supported by four legs; and by order of the sheriff placed on the State House square. Hither the prisoner was conducted, and being previously well booted and spurred by the officer, was mounted on the oaken stud. Here he continued for half an hour, laughing at his own fate, and making diversion for a numerous body of spectators who honored him with their company. After this part of the sentence had been legally and faithfully executed, the culprit was dismounted and led to the whipping post, where the duties made him more serious. The whole was performed with great order and regularity."

While women were not made to suffer the indignity of riding the wooden horse, they were sometimes stripped to the waist and flogged, either at a cart's tail or at the public whipping post. This punishment survived in New England into the nineteenth century. Here is an eye-witness account of the whipping of a woman at Newfane, Vermont, from the history of that town. It is distressing to think that children were permitted to witness these horrid spectacles.

"At an early period corporal punishment was inflicted at every term of Court on Newfane Hill. The writer, when a mere boy, remembers witnessing the whipping of Old Mother White of Wardsboro, in August 1807. She was convicted of passing counterfeit money, and sentenced to receive thirty lashes upon her bare back. A great crowd of men and women collected to witness the whipping. The Post was in the form of a cross, with a transverse strip near the top, to which her bare arms were bound, and her body was stripped to the waist. The High Sheriff applied a certain number of stripes, and the balance was allotted to his Deputies, some seven in number, and some of whom applied the blows with great vigor. Near the close of the whipping her back became raw, and she suffered excessive pain and shrieked and screamed terribly in her agony. The writer, although very young, remembers the scene distinctly. The Meeting House and the Academy stood a few rods above the site of the Whipping Post, and the windows were filled with women, gazing intently on the revolting scene. This was probably the last woman publicly whipped in Vermont, for the Legislature abolished the Whipping Post that fall and provided for the building of a States Prison at Windsor."

On August 11, 1789, eleven culprits received the discipline of the post in Boston, but the man who wielded the whip did not have his heart in the work. "The person obtained by the High Sheriff to inflict the punishment, from sympathetick feeling for his brother culprits, was very tender in dealing out his strokes, and not adding weight to them, although repeatedly ordered; the Sheriff, to his honor, took the whip from his hand, by an application of it to his shoulders drove him from the stage, and with the assistance of his Deputies inflicted the punishment of the law on all the culprits. The citizens who were assembled, complimented the Sheriff with three cheers for the manly, determined manner in which he executed his duty."

This whipping of the whipper recalls the poetic justice of the early case of Edward Palmer, who for his extortion in taking thirty-three shillings seven pence for the plank and woodwork of the Boston stocks was fined five pounds and ordered to be set an hour in the stocks.

No class of offenses was looked after more sharply by our ancestors than offenses of the tongue. Philip Ratcliffe of the colony was sentenced to "be whipped, have his ears cut off, fined forty shillings, and banished out of the limits of the jurisdiction, for uttering malicious and scandalous speeches against the government and court of Salem."

The "prophanely behaved" person who tarried "without dores att the meeting-house on the Lord's daies" to indulge in social talk, was "admonished" by the constables; on a second offense he was "sett in the stockes," and if his moral sense remained warped, he was brought before the courts. The person who had the temerity to interrupt the preacher, or falsely charge the minister with error "in the open face of the church," or otherwise made "God's ways contemptible and ridiculous, every such person or persons (whatsoever censure the church may passe) shall for the first scandall be convented and reproved openly by the magistrate at some Lecture, and bound to their good behaviour. And if the second time they break forthe into like contemptuous carriages, they shall either pay five pounds to the publique Treasure or stand two houres openly upon a block or stoole four foot high upon a Lecture day, with a paper fixed on his Breast written with capitalle letters, AN OPEN AND OBSTINATE CONTEMNER OF GOD'S HOLY ORDINANCES."

The ducking stool was a special form of punishment for women. Its use in New England seems to have been generally confined to Massachusetts, where its salutary effects as a remedy against the nuisance of a scolding woman's tongue were so much appreciated that it flourished for many years.

"Scolds," says Josselyn, writing of the Old Body of Laws of 1646, "they gag and set them at their doors for certain hours, for all comers and goers by to gaze at."

In the court records of Hartford County, Connecticut, will be found the earliest trace and peculiar use of the once familiar phrase, "God bless you over the left shoulder," or, more briefly, "Over the left."

"At a County Court held at Hartford
"September 4, 1795

"Whereas James Steel did commence an action against Bevell Waters (both of Hartford) in this Court, upon hearing and tryall whereof the Court gave judgment against said Waters, (as in justice they think they ought,) upon the declaring the said judgment, the said Waters did review to the Court in March next, that, being granted and entered, the said Waters, as he departed from the table he said, *'God bless you over the left shoulder.'*

"The Court ordered a record to be made thereof forthwith.

"A true copie: Test.
"Caleb Stanley, Clerk."

At the next court, Waters was tried for contempt, for saying the words recited, "so cursing the Court," and on verdict fined £5. He asked a review of the Court following, which was granted; and, pending trial, the Court asked counsel of the Reverend Messrs. Woodbridge and Buckingham, the ministers of the Hartford churches, as to the "common acceptation" of the offensive phrase. Here is their reply:

"We are of opinion that those words, said on the other side to be spoken by Bevell Waters, include (1) prophaness, by using the name of God, that is holy, with such

ill words to which it was joyned; (2) that they carry great
contempt in them, arising to the degree of an imprecation
or curse, the words of a curse being the most contemptible
that can ordinarily be used.

"T. Woodbridge.
"T. Buckingham

"March 7th, 1795-6."

The former judgment was affirmed on review.

The church took a strong hand in correcting wrong-
doers. Our Puritan ancestors tried to regulate their conduct according to scriptural precepts. With them there
was never any question that authority to punish offense
was vested in the church. Discipline was the name given
to the ecclesiastical punishment of transgressors, and it

was, so far as humiliation and disgrace were concerned, worse for the unfortunate offender than if he were to find himself in a court of law.

Discipline lasted for generations in the New England churches. A sensational church trial which packed the galleries of an East Boston meeting house in 1860 was reported by the *Boston Herald* as follows:

"For the past two weeks, the religious community of East Boston has been interested by a church trial, one of the members of the church having been accused of having intercourse with his half sister, a girl fourteen or fifteen years old, and also charged with beating her unmercifully. From the testimony that was offered, it appeared that the old wretch used to have intercourse with the girl and afterward beat her, as a relief to his conscience, for consenting. It also appeared that if she refused to gratify his passion, he would beat her, sometimes stripping her clothes entirely from her body, and lashing her with pieces of rope and sticks, and generally once a day.

"At length the sisters and brothers of the church put their heads together and concluded to give the old scamp a church trial, and after the admission of much evidence, he was found guilty of both counts, and is to be expelled from the church."

Connecticut once had a lady horse thief named Abby Jane who was guilty of a novel crime. One has heard of convicts breaking out of prison, but this daring young creature broke into prison. Convicted of horse stealing in 1853, she was sentenced to four years in the state's prison at Wethersfield. She served out her term and was discharged, with the usual cash present of two dollars given at that time by the state to departing felons.

Now, Abby could not get very far on that sum, so she

lingered in Wethersfield, where she soon found a job doing housework. For a while she seems to have behaved herself, but presently her old pilfering habits returned, and she was detected by the family for whom she worked. Abby left, but returned secretly, and stole a horse blanket from General Welles. With the stolen blanket for a bed and coverlid, she took lodgings under the general's barn floor, remaining there during the day and coming out at night to milk the neighborhood cows and forage for food. Living under the barn was a lonely life, and after a few days Abby began to feel homesick for her old prison home. She scaled the prison wall by climbing a tree and dropping into the yard of the women's section, where she hid in the rubbish of the woodpile.

Her old cronies were surprised and delighted to have her back and supplied her with food. After four or five days, during which Abby stole supplies whenever possible, she took up her residence in an old ash hole or oven. The matron, who had missed provisions and other articles, was greatly puzzled, and a general search was made. The warden, pulling out some pieces of refuse stove piping from under the oven, beheld the once fair face of Abby Jane peering at him from under the sooty canopy. Crawling out of the kennel, Abby once more found herself a prisoner. She was not indicted, however, for illegally entering the prison, but was sentenced to a year in jail for stealing. Soon after her release she broke into a dwelling, stealing, besides other goods and chattels, a pair of pantaloons containing five hundred dollars. And the last trace I have of Abby, she was waiting to be tried for this offense, with every prospect of a speedy return to her old quarters at the state's prison.

The Self-Destructive Townsmen

PELHAM, Massachusetts, is one of New England's unsung towns. It stands forlorn and weathered on the range of hills that lies along the easterly side of the Connecticut Valley above Springfield. Its immediate neighbor to the north is Shutesbury, the town of which it used to be said that the inhabitants raised huckleberries in summer and hell in winter; while along much of its southern border lies Belchertown, a name which suggests the place may once have been the home of a volcano, that belched fire and smoke and rumbled terribly, though it was in fact christened in honor of one of its colonial proprietors, Governor Jonathan Belcher of Massachusetts. Both Shutesbury and Belchertown are attractive hilltop towns, but Pelham is a dusty hangover from another world.

Yet of all the top-deck towns in this region, Pelham has by far the most interesting history. The town hall, which stands foursquare on the top of Pelham Hill without any make-up on its facade, has the aged-in-the-wood look of an old wine cask. Actually, it is the oldest town hall in consecutive use in Massachusetts. It was built in 1743, the year Pelham was incorporated as a town, though the place was first settled by Scotch Presbyterians from Worcester four years earlier. For more than two hundred years the people of Pelham have gathered here in town meeting to discuss not only parochial matters but also every war this country has engaged in from the French and Indian Wars to World War II. It was the storm center of the three leading events in the history of the town—events of a very strange and extraordinary character—namely, the pastorate of the godless adventurer, Stephen Burroughs; the revolt of the western Massachusetts farmers under the leadership of Captain Daniel Shays of Pelham; and the repeated attempts of the town to commit suicide by voting itself out of existence.

The first of these events goes back to a spring day in the year 1784, when a young man nineteen years old, dressed in a light blue-gray coat with silver-plated buttons, a green vest, and red velvet knee breeches, rode up the hill into Pelham. This youth was Stephen Burroughs, whose exploits were to gain him widespread notoriety as one of the most infamous characters in the country. He was a thief, a counterfeiter, an impostor, and a seducer. The son of a New Hampshire Presbyterian minister, he ran away from home at fourteen to join the Continental Army, but because of his youth was kept out of the fighting. Disappointed in not seeing any action, he returned home, with his discharge from the army secured. Then for two years he was a student at Dartmouth College, from which he was expelled for an undergraduate prank involving the theft of some honey. When he was seventeen he went to sea as a ship's doctor on a voyage to France, after being coached in the rudiments of medicine by a regular practitioner. Next he tried his hand at teaching, but lost his job when a Dartmouth tutor told the people in the village where Burroughs kept school that he was not a proper person to entrust with the education of their children. Back home once more, he decided to try preaching and, stuffing ten old manuscript sermons of his father's into his saddlebags, mounted his horse and rode away. Hearing that the pulpit at Pelham was vacant, he turned in that direction and was presently climbing Pelham Hill in the character of a preacher.

"What a pretty fellow am I for a preacher!" he said. "A pretty character, mine, to tickle the ears of a grave audience! Run away from my own home for being connected in robbing a bee house, and for my attention to a married woman; having been through scenes of tumult, during my whole career."

Despite his clothes' being more flamboyant than those usually worn by clergymen, who customarily dressed in black, Burroughs, who now called himself the Reverend Mr. Davis, succeeded in persuading the pillars of the Pelham church to hire him for a month. He was to be paid five dollars a Sunday and receive food and lodging for himself and keep for his horse. The Pelham Presbyterians were not easy to please, and it speaks well for the sermons which Burroughs stole from his father, to say nothing of his own delivery of them, that when he had preached four Sundays he was re-engaged for sixteen more. But that he had ability of his own as a preacher is shown by an incident that occurred during his Pelham pastorate. Called upon at short notice to preach at a funeral in a home, he took along one of his father's sermons. Some of his parishioners who were in a position to look over his shoulder could not help seeing that he was using a dog-eared manuscript written in faded ink. They became suspicious and at last decided to test Burroughs by giving him a text from which to preach just as he was entering the pulpit on Sunday morning. This was done, but Burroughs acquitted himself in fine style, not forgetting to give his auditors a sharp thrust or two during his discourse.

Then the inevitable happened. When he had been in Pelham nearly five months, with only one Sunday left to preach, but hoping to be retained, some one from Dartmouth College met and recognized him. Burroughs tried to bluff this person into thinking he had mistaken his identity, but his bluff was called, and Burroughs knew the jig was up. That night he fled.

The next day, when the people learned they had been duped by an impostor, they were so indignant that they raised a hue and cry against him and started immediately in pursuit. This was something which Burroughs had not counted on. For they caught up with him in the near-by town of Rutland, Massachusetts, where they chased him into a barn. Armed with a scythe snath, Burroughs defied them from the top of the haymow, and no one dared go up after him, lest he mow the person down. Perhaps they were awed at seeing their late pastor suddenly standing at bay ready to fight the whole pack of pursuers. A pamphlet, now a rarity, called *The Hay Mow Sermon*, is alleged to contain the discourse Burroughs delivered in the barn to the outraged Pelhamites; but he does not himself mention this sermon in his book, *Memoirs of the Notorious Stephen Burroughs of New Hampshire*, and it is probably a spurious production. The Rutlanders, who had looked on in amazement, learning that the chief complaint against

Burroughs was that he had not delivered a sermon for which he had been paid five dollars, suggested that he settle by standing drinks at the tavern, which suggestion proved agreeable to both sides.

The venerable town hall on Pelham Hill was at that time also the meeting house, and it was in this same building that Stephen Burroughs preached for nineteen Sundays. Inside, it is not quite the same as it was, for about 1840 a floor was laid between the galleries, giving the place an additional room.

Outside the ancient building, a block of granite recalls the second outstanding event in Pelham's history. The inscription on this stone reads:

To Commemorate
Daniel Shays
Captain in the American Revolution
Leader of the Shays Rebellion
Against Unjust Laws
On this Hilltop Half of His Ragged Army
Encamped for Six Nights Jan 28 to Feb 3 1787
Erected 1936

Daniel Shays was not a native of Pelham, nor is it known for certain where and when he was born, but tradition says the place was Hopkinton, Massachusetts, and the year 1747. His parents were poor, and Daniel seems to have had little schooling. He grew up into a towering man as brawny as a blacksmith, and in the Revolution proved himself to be a brave-hearted and tireless soldier. His first soldiering was done in April, 1775, when as a Minuteman he sniped at the British returning from Concord. He distinguished himself at Bunker Hill, winning a promotion. He was at Ticonderoga, Saratoga, and Stony

Point. On New Year's day, 1777, he was commissioned a captain in the Fifth Massachusetts regiment. In 1780 he resigned his commission and settled at Pelham, occupying a small, one-story, hillside farmhouse that was not much better than a shack.

The short-lived period of prosperity that followed the war was succeeded by hard times that bore especially heavily on the farmers. The Continental currency was, to use a phrase still in circulation, not worth a continental, and the want of a circulating medium produced a general train of difficulties which were made worse by severe land taxes. Farmers were crushed under a mountain of debt owed to the mercantile classes, and the lawyers did a land-office business stripping them in the courts of everything they had, and then throwing them neck and crop off their farms. The farmers were desperate, but their protests and pleas brought no relief from the state government. It began to look to them as if the Revolution which was fought to establish their rights had been waged in vain. During 1786 there were many meetings of angry farmers in the western counties and in other parts of the state. And Captain Daniel Shays, who in his dire poverty had been forced to sell the treasured sword presented to him by Lafayette, began drilling men in Pelham.

Late in the year 1786, Shays, at the head of three hundred armed malcontents, marched into Springfield, seized the courthouse, and prevented the court from sitting. Shays's poverty-stricken farmers probably felt as Jack Cade and his rebels did when they entered London. Shakespeare gives one of them the line, "The first thing we do, let's kill all the lawyers." Action similar to that at Springfield was taken at other places in Massachusetts; American history repeated itself more than one hundred and fifty years later during the hard times of President Hoover's administration, when the farmers of Iowa took possession of courthouses in that state to stop the foreclosure of farm mortgages. The situation in Massachusetts had gone so far that the governor and council decided to call out troops to put down the insurrection in the western

General Benjamin Lincoln

counties. A force of 4,400 militia under command of General Benjamin Lincoln was ordered under arms. Half of these troops were to report to General Lincoln at Roxbury, now part of Boston, on January 19, 1787, while General Shepard was ordered to take command at Springfield and collect troops there.

Capture of the government arsenal at Springfield was essential to the insurgent cause, as many of Shays's men were armed only with pitchforks, and it was plain that their chances of success would be greater if the attempt was made before the arrival of General Lincoln and his men. Consequently, Shays began concentrating his forces around Springfield. Four hundred men under Luke Day were stationed across the Connecticut River in West Springfield; four hundred more from the Berkshires under Levi Parsons were at Chicopee, and Shays himself with a force of eleven hundred was near the Boston road. Hearing that General Lincoln was well on the way to Springfield, Shays decided to attack the arsenal on January 25. He wrote to Day to co-operate with him. Day, in a letter which was intercepted by General Shepard, replied that he could not support Shays on the twenty-fifth but would do so the following day.

Shays, in ignorance of this and counting on Day's support, marched into Springfield. To defend the arsenal, General Shepard had quickly collected nine hundred men, later augmented by two hundred more, so that the opposing forces were about equal in numbers, though Shepard's men were well armed and provided with ordnance. Shays, with his troops in open column, approached the arsenal about four o'clock in the afternoon. General Shepard sent messengers several times to ask what their intentions were and to warn them of their danger. The answer given was that they would have the arsenal, and they advanced to within two hundred and fifty yards. General Shepard then sent word that he was there by order of the governor and Congress and if they came any nearer he would open fire.

"That is all we want," said one of the rebel leaders. They then advanced another hundred yards. Compelled at last to fire, General Shepard ordered the first two rounds to be fired over their heads, but instead of intimidating the rebels this only quickened their advance, and the cannons were then brought to bear on the center of the column. It was a moment charged with drama. Then suddenly the cry of murder was raised at the rear of Shays's men, which threw the whole body into a panic. Shays tried desperately to rally and reform them, but it was no use. They fled to Ludlow ten miles away, leaving three of their comrades dead and one wounded on the field. General Shepard could have pursued and cut many to pieces, but his idea was not to kill them but to bring them to their senses.

Despite this routing of the insurgents, there was still the possibility that they might try again to take the arsenal. Day with his command was still in West Springfield, and Parsons at Chicopee. Shays, who lost about two hundred men by desertion, joined forces with the latter the next day. But whatever fears Shepard may have felt, were relieved at noon on the twenty-sixth by the arrival of General Lincoln.

Shays retreated up the Connecticut Valley to Hadley, then swung eastward to Pelham, arriving there January 28. Half of his scarecrow army bivouacked on top of Pelham Hill near the town hall. This was about as cold and exposed a situation as could be found, but perhaps it was a good defensive position. The rest of his men were in a more sheltered place under the hill to the eastward, where Shays had his headquarters at a lonely public house called Conkey's Tavern that was an old hangout of his. The arrival of eleven sleigh-loads of provisions helped to cheer the weary and dispirited men, and they remained at Pelham nearly a week.

Meanwhile, General Lincoln lost little time in taking up Shays's trail. On February 3, while one of Shays's lieutenants was parleying with one of Lincoln's officers, the insurgents moved from Pelham to Petersham. General

Lincoln, who was at Hadley with his army, hearing of Shays's withdrawal, started after him. He began the march at eight o'clock in the evening. By two in the morning his troops had reached New Salem. It was an intensely cold night, with a strong north wind, and at New Salem they ran into a snowstorm. The route lay over hills where they were exposed to the full force of the weather, but, hampered as they were by these conditions, they pressed on through the night, covering the thirty miles to Petersham in one of the most remarkable forced marches made in this country. Lincoln's front reached Petersham at nine in the morning, while the rear troops were five miles away. The surprise of the insurgents was complete. They fled in confusion from the town without putting up any resistance. They were pursued in the snow for two miles, and one hundred and fifty of them were captured. Many of the fugitives went home, while the ringleaders fled to New Hampshire, Vermont, and New York. Shays was among those who escaped. He was excepted from the general amnesty granted soon afterward to the participants in the insurrection, and the Supreme Court condemned him to death for treason. Fourteen were sentenced to die, but all were pardoned, including Shays. "Popular sympathies for the uprising remained so strong," says Charles A. Beard, "that the state officials did not dare execute Shays or any of his followers."

In May following the insurrection the convention that framed the United States Constitution met in Philadelphia.

One gets the impression that Shays was a sincere and courageous man who, though personally popular with his followers, was lacking in any real qualities of leadership. He moved away from Pelham, eventually settling in

Sparta, New York, where during his latter years he enjoyed a pension from the federal government for his military services during the Revolution. He died at Sparta in 1825.

The attempts that were made by the people of Pelham to destroy the town politically and dismember the corporate body were not because of chagrin over being victimized by Stephen Burroughs or shame at having been a hotbed of rebellion in the days of Daniel Shays. Neither was it done from any desire to live in a state of unrestrained and wanton freedom, as was the case with the fisher folk at the Isles of Shoals off the New Hampshire coast, who burned their church, abandoned their local government, and became terribly bestialized and degraded. Pelham's first attempt at self-destruction was not made until 1854.

To understand the reasons for this unusual action, it is necessary to take note of certain physical facts which have affected Pelham's life from the beginning. It is an uneven, rocky township of scattered farms occupying a long, high ridge of land rising nearly a thousand feet above the valleys on either side. On the easterly side the drop is at the rate of about nine hundred feet in two miles. This is a sparsely settled section of the township. It should perhaps be stated that the part of Prescott formerly flanking Pelham on the easterly side, and the town of Enfield which touched it at the southeast corner, now lie at the bottom of the vast Quabbin Reservoir.

On the western side of Pelham Hill one descends some nine hundred feet in less than five miles into the Connecticut Valley. This part of Pelham is bordered by the town of Amherst and is watered by the Fort River, which flows into the Connecticut. Here were the best farms and

the village of West Pelham. The natural market and center for the people residing on this side of Pelham was
Amherst, which was nearer and easier to reach than Pelham Center, at the top of a long uphill climb, where there
really wasn't much of anything except the church and the
post office. As far back as the early part of the nineteenth
century, farmers living along the border next to Amherst
wanted to be set off to that town, or at least be permitted
to attend church there. But the rest of Pelham did not
wish to lose any of its prosperous citizens, as this would
have increased the burden of those left to maintain roads,
provide schools, and support the poor. Never a rich town,
Pelham had more paupers than any other place in that
part of Massachusetts. It was the people dwelling on the
sunset side of the town that were most anxious to extin-
guish it.

To be, or not to be: that was the question which faced
the people of Pelham when they met in special session in
the town hall on January 31, 1854. The purpose of the
meeting was thus stated in the death warrant:

"To see if said Town is willing to give up and surrender her town Charter and become disfranchised as to all
privileges and rights.

"To act on the subject of having said Town divided in
any legal way and manner and having the parts annexed to
adjoining towns, and to use any legal means to accomplish
the same."

Sparks flew as senior voices were raised for and against
the proposal. The lowlanders from the western part of the
town were in favor of surrender, the highlanders opposed
to it. Both sides were present in force. When the vote was
finally taken, it was decided "to surrender this Town's
Charter according to the warrant calling this meeting."

There were 73 in favor of dissolution, 36 against it. Committees were immediately chosen to urge favorable consideration by the legislature, to circulate petitions in Pelham endorsing the action taken, and to influence public opinion for merger in the surrounding towns.

Poor Pelham, however, was promptly rebuffed by its neighbors. Nobody wanted any part of it. Amherst went on record at a special town meeting held February 24, 1854, with a resolution passed by a vote of 168 to 84 which read as follows:

"Resolved: as the sense of the Town of Amherst, that as at present advised, and in the present state of proceedings before the Legislature, on the petition of the Town of Pelham for leave to surrender its Charter, and to be annexed to the adjoining towns, we are opposed to the surrender of its Charter, and to annexation of any part of its territory to the Town of Amherst."

Instructions were given to the town's legislative representative at Boston to oppose the Pelham petition.

This was dampening to the spirits of the Pelhamites favoring disintegration. With the time for the annual town meeting drawing near, it was decided to reconsider the question, and accordingly an article was included in the warrant for the meeting, to see if the town would rescind the vote to surrender its charter. This brought out an even larger crowd than the special meeting. At that meeting a total of 109 votes were cast, but at the annual meeting the number was 171, and the attempt to rescind was defeated by the narrow margin of 87 to 84. Since women did not vote and allowance must be made for the number of children and young people of nonvoting age in Pelham, which then had a population of 789, the total must have been pretty nearly the full voting strength of the town.

In view of Amherst's action, the matter was permitted to drift along for a couple of years until January, 1856, when it was decided to sound out the sentiment of the town again. A special meeting was called at which the people reversed their previous verdict, voting against surrender 73 to 36.

For the next decade, which included the period of the Civil War, no official action was taken, but in 1867 the controversy was revived. Surrender was again overruled 45 to 43.

One must admire the persistence of the extinctionists. Their final and most determined effort came in 1870. At the town meeting of March 15 the warrant contained this article: "To see if the town consents to surrender its charter and divide its territory between the towns of Amherst, Prescott, Enfield, and Belchertown as already petitioned for to the Legislature by citizens of the town of Pelham and also to designate lines of Division."

The record reads, "Voted: that we Surrender our Charter—86 in favor; 36 against."

Amherst and Prescott reacted quickly with special meetings at which both towns gave Pelham the cold shoulder. Prescott had almost as many paupers as Pelham and did not want to be saddled with any more. Amherst would probably have been willing to annex a few fat farms, but did not wish to extend its borders to include extensive tracts of less desirable land. Pelham's neighbors opposed the liquidation in the legislature, where the petition presented by the Pelham selectmen was referred to the Committee on Towns. The committee reported adversely on it, whereupon the legislature gave the selectmen leave to withdraw.

The fight, however, did not end quite there. Pelham was represented by a resourceful politician who was strongly in favor of dissolution and merger. He persuaded the legislature to pass an order reading, "That the Committee on the Judiciary inquire whether the town of Pelham has a legal existence, it having voted to surrender its charter."

This was on May 15, 1870, and a week later the Judiciary Committee reported back, "That, in the opinion of the Committee, no town can vote to surrender its charter and dissolve its corporate existence, without the consent of the legislature, had and received. A town is the creature of the law, and has only the powers given by statute, and among these is not the power of annulling its existence. Its general powers are to provide schools, maintain highways, protect the lives and property of its citizens and support its paupers; its general duties are to furnish its part of the State tax, its quota of soldiers, etc., etc.; it is, in fact, an intermediate agent between the State government and the people. And as it is strictly limited to the powers conferred by statute, and as the town of Pelham has not the power of surrendering its charter without the consent of the legislature given it by statute, and as it clearly cannot relieve itself of the obligations imposed upon it without such consent, the Committee are unanimously of the opinion that the town of Pelham has a legal existence, any of its votes to the contrary notwithstanding."

Here ended the attempts of the town of Pelham to give up the ghost. George H. Haynes, who half a century ago investigated this queer chapter in Pelham's history and wrote about it in the *Journal of the American Antiquarian*

Society, says that the day following the vote in the legislature refusing dissolution there was a regularly summoned town meeting at which appropriations were made and other routine matters of local government attended to as if nothing had happened. During his investigation, Mr. Haynes, to whose research I am indebted for much of the material used here, found a letter at the State House in Boston from the town clerk of Pelham which flashes a revealing beam on town affairs. The letter, which was dated January 27, 1873, was written in answer to a request that the town reports be filed in the state archives. Here in part is what the clerk said:

"I do not think our town affairs are in such shape or have been for the years 1870 & 1 that a report could be made thay doo not Know how much thay are in debt much more than you do whare thay have borrowed the money thay keep no Account of it on book as can be found and ther is interest money cauled for that has not Ben paid for 3 or 4 years and in fact our Board of Selectmen New nothing about

"Perhaps i am Saying to much But Such are the facts.
"Yours Respectfully
"Clerk of the Town of Pelham, Mass."

Happily, Pelham still lives, but, like many hill towns in western Massachusetts, it has lost population and has today fewer inhabitants than it had a century ago. There are perhaps five hundred souls there now, whereas, as we have seen, there were nearly eight hundred in 1870. It seems to have reached its peak about 1820, when it was credited with a population of 1,278. This figure was cut down two years later when the eastern part of Pelham was taken to create the new town of Prescott. Pelham is a place of wide horizons, and in the past people looking off to the hills got to thinking that perhaps they could do better elsewhere, and some of these restless persons drifted away. If, as some have declared, Pelham is the most forlorn town in New England, then the second most forsaken one is Halifax, Vermont. Like Pelham, it perches high on a windy hill, and, curious to relate, it was settled by Pelham people. From this elevated town came Otis the elevator man.

The last time I saw Pelham was on an Indian summer day. I went there by way of Belchertown, with its bandstand on the green, driving up Pelham Hill by the same route Stephen Burroughs took when he first rode his horse into town, wearing his light blue coat with the silver-plated buttons, his green vest, and his red velvet knee breeches. There was a purple haze on the hills, and it seemed to me to be the most agreeable region in the world. Surely it was the visual glory of the surrounding country that led the early Pelhamites to build their meeting house on the hill.

On Pelham Hill today there is not even a filling station. Beside the town hall is the abandoned church that was built in 1837. It is ballasted with great blocks of local granite in its foundations. From the same quarry, perhaps, came the stone doorstep of the town hall. Across the way is an old farmhouse, and down the road is another. Pelham has eleven cemeteries, but the burial ground behind the town hall is the oldest. It is like an ancient stonewalled pasture full of mossy gray stones. Here I found wintergreen and bluebells growing among the graves. I also found the tombstone of the Reverend Robert Abercrombie, who drank the committee of church elders under the table when they came to remonstrate with him about his drinking habits, as related elsewhere in this book. The roll of honor of World War II before the Town Hall showed a long list of names, but reading it on that lonely hilltop with hardly a house in sight I wondered whence they all came. Dropping down the hill into the pleasant village of West Pelham, however, I met with ample signs of life.

It is here that the old fish-pole factory is situated, nestling on the side of a ravine. For many years this industry flourished, turning out all kinds of expertly fashioned rods for those who follow the tranquilizing pursuit of angling. Hundreds of different styles were made for fresh- and salt-water fishermen. Pelham rods enjoyed an excellent reputation. I had hoped to find the factory still in operation, but I was fourteen or fifteen years too late.

"It was taken over by the Montague Fishing Rod Company," an elderly Pelham gentleman told me. "The machinery and equipment were moved to Montague. They're using it up there. Make good rods, they do."

It is pleasant to think amid the crowds, the clamor, and the confusion of modern life that peaceful old New England towns like Pelham still exist. I for one hope Pelham will never pass to extinction; at least, not until I have been able to visit it at night, to view the ancient town hall and the abandoned church on the hilltop under a gibbous moon.

Live Yankees From
a Town History

Town histories belong to a class of books which make delightful reading. Written usually by someone who knows and loves the place of which he writes, and written for those who also know and love it, these books possess a warmth and native flavor often absent from books by writers who are not so completely at home in their subjects.

Anyone who wishes to become the author of a book that will be read one hundred years from now should write a history of his own home town. It is the surest passport to literary immortality, because no matter how obscure and unimportant the town, there will always be people who will want to read about it. Robert Southey had an inkling of this when in the midst of writing the volumes of his Portuguese history he suddenly had misgivings. How much better it would have been, he said, had he written the history of the street wherein he was born, recording the changes that had taken place there during the years he had known it.

Since there are various practical ways of getting a town history published, the writing of one may solve the problem of the man who wants to write but has nowhere to print, and also that of the person who wants to write but lacks a subject. Even if the history of a town has been written, there is usually room for a supplemental volume bringing the record down to date.

A few years ago an historically minded citizen of Bath, Maine, left $5,000 to have the history of his city written from the time the last historian left off—$3,000 for printing expenses, $2,000 for the author. He nominated for the job a local newspaper editor who was about to retire, and the book was written with the happiest results. Men will come and go, but the book will remain a splendid memorial to the man who made it possible and his friend who wrote it.

Excellent town histories have been written by both men and women, but a town should have its history written at least twice, once by a man and once by a woman, because each knows more and writes better about some things than the other. Collaboration is inadvisable; the result seldom lives up to expectations.

Probably the most unsatisfactory town history is the one written by divers hands. When many people are invited to contribute the result is usually a hasty pudding spoiled by too many cooks. Once the editor asks local people to write something, he is bound to take it all and cannot hurt the contributors' feelings by throwing their stuff overboard, though it may be very bad indeed. An enterprising lady I know, who undertook the editorship of a town history by a coalition of local scribes, found herself the editor of an anthology of poetry, as most of the contributions were in verse. The whole town burst into song.

But if the poetry was bad, the pictures collected for the book were good. Frequently they are the best part of a town history. In the books about the coastal towns there are usually pictures of ships and sometimes even ship-wrecks and magnificent old skippers in throat whiskers. Extremely interesting are the patriarchal photographs of family reunions in the period following the Civil War, showing five generations sitting on settees under the apple trees or grouped around the doorstep of the ancestral home. Very interesting, too, are the period pictures of town meetings of yesteryear, with all the oldest male in-habitants present, and views of Main Street about 1860, when there were horses and top-buggies and citizens in top hats and unpressed pants. The topographical photo-graphs, both landscape and architecture, are generally successful because they were taken in the days before pho-tography was considered an art. A person bent on pho-tographing the local waterfall or the Epaphroditus Jones house simply walked straight up to the place and took an honest picture of it, without feeling obliged to crawl under a bush to get a worm's-eye view, or insisting on the branches of a tree overhanging the foreground. But best of all are the portraits, especially of the women, some of which are from daguerreotypes. The town histories of New England comprise the finest family photograph al-bum or series of albums in America.

One soon learns how to read town histories—the big books about little places. I always skip the geological and genealogical chapters, especially the former when they go back to as remote a source as the Flood, and the latter when they read like the Bible, with Ezra marrying Mind-

well and begetting little Hiram who dies in infancy. But if
the genealogical section contains notes about the people
listed, I read it, because you never can tell what will come
to light. I recall reading about the matriarch of a family

who died en route to America while a passenger in one of
the early ships. As the ship was nearing land, they did not
bury her at sea, but stowed her in her chest, and when they
brought her ashore for burial she fooled them all at the
grave by sitting up. When I asked one of her descendants
about the incident, he said, "Sure, I've got the chest."

Professional historians may sniff at these parochial productions, charging the town chronicler with inability to disengage rumor from fact, but the very character of the gossip and legends once current in a community helps in presenting a picture of the life of the place. The local pride and prejudice may be strong, but one of the best views you can get of people is in the town histories of a region.

In proof of this the following extracts are offered without comment from the *History of Sutton from 1704-1878*. Sutton is a town in Worcester County, Massachusetts. Evidently, in a spirit of patriotism the town planned to publish its history in 1876, the centennial year of American independence, but something went wrong, and it did not appear until 1878, after two ministers, Reverend William A. Benedict and Reverend Hiram A. Tracy, had taken over the project. These gentlemen did as thorough a job as they knew how. Devoting one section to the homes of Sutton, they systematically covered every house in town, telling who built it, who had lived there, and anything of interest that they could learn about the inmates. It is from this part of the book that most of the excerpts which follow have been taken.

"Aaron Elliot, Jr., was a scythe maker, and his scythes were genuine, of the best temper. He could not only make a scythe, but he knew how to use one. He swung a scythe four feet long, and no one attempted to out-mow him. He mowed an acre, on a wager, quicker than an expert could rake it. He was athletic. He said that when he was sixteen years old, the water being hard at the house, they had to bring water for washing from a well some twenty rods away. So he took a common cider barrel, of thirty-two gallons capacity, down to the well, filled it with water, drove in the bung, shouldered the barrel, took the wooden funnel in one hand, and carried them both to the house."

"Pliny Slocumb was one of the assessors in this town. He was a Freemason, belonged to the Sutton Lyceum, and was skilled in debate. He was an artist, an ornamental painter, and one of the fastest workmen to be found. His sleighs, chairs, cradles, settees, etc., were much sought after for their fanciful ornamentation. One of his sons, too, was an artist, and painted a panorama, with which he traveled. Mr. Slocumb gave some attention to fruit growing, and made choice wines, on which he realized a handsome profit."

"Staunton was an eccentric genius, a cordwainer or shoemaker by trade. He used to go round 'whipping the cat' as they styled it; i.e., making boots and shoes for families in their own houses. He was noted for his odd sayings. His last sickness was in the winter. He was not quite ready to go, so he said, 'If God will spare me now, I will make Him the best pair of boots that He ever had; it is too bad to have to die after living through such a winter.' But alas his attempted bribe availed him not."

"There used to be a house up in the lot owned and occupied by Widow Wakefield and her son Joseph; she was noted for her eccentricities.

"She kept many cats, and to feed them caught fish. While angling one day she drew a large pickerel out of the water, when by a sudden flop it broke the hook and left, when she exclaimed, 'O the laws! How desputly it makes a body feel to lose what they never had!' She wore a large pocket and would fill it with fish, and then come home and feed her score of cats, calling each by name and giving it a fish as it came forth. One young man killed seventeen of her cats one night, laying them all in a row on a large stone. The old lady finding them there the next morning called on God to curse the killer. So he having bad luck in after life laid it to the widow's curse.

"Some one stole some of Joe's chickens, so he took the rest to roost on the headboard of his bed, instructing them to sit with their beaks toward him. He once went in a boat on Manchaug Pond, and caught a pickerel that weighed five and a half pounds; it so surprised him that his shouts were heard on Putnam Hill and at the Waters' place; the people, thinking him in the pond, ran to his assistance, when he said, 'O the goddies! Who can beat that?' "

"Simon Keith has been treasurer and collector of this town, and was constable for several years. Mrs. Keith left his bed while he was asleep, went down and fell into the well, where she was drowned August 5, 1860. Her fall awoke her husband, who went to her assistance, but she died before he could get her out of the water. Whether she was asleep or awake when the accident happened, no one knows. Charity would suggest somnambulism."

"In the days of the Revolution a train of powder wagons accompanied by a military escort, on its way from Philadelphia to Boston, passed this house. One of the Whites' boys, full of mischief, stuck pitch pine slivers into an apple, and as the train passed, lighted his torch and threw it at the last powder cart, which act so enraged the guard, that they came back to the house, broke out all the windows and threatened the lives of the tenants, thinking them Tories. One woman with a child in her arms was obliged to run for her life, the guard threatening to pierce her with his sword if she did not leave. She ran to the Elder Waters' house, and the boy to save his life went and hid under the flume at the mill. After hunting a long time for the boy they went to Le Baron's Tavern, where they spent the night; and when they threatened to go back and burn the house, feeling sure that Tories lived there, Mr. Le Baron's assurance that they were good Union people, and that it was only the foolish act of a mischievous boy, was all that saved the house."

"Mr. Le Baron commenced keeping tavern in an old house which was standing when he bought the place. He built the present large and commodious house about 1794. His tavern was considered the most popular between Boston and Hartford, and was constantly thronged by visitors. He used to mention among the distinguished guests he had entertained, General Lafayette, Governor John Hancock, Major Paul Jones, General Putnam and others. He kept a store and did quite an extensive business.

"Tradition has handed down the following amusing anecdote: He closed the store one day, and left, taking the key with him. Soon after a customer came for something, but could not get in; so his daughter, a heavy, buxom girl, said she could get in and get what he wanted. She placed a ladder under the attic window, and went in. From the attic she had to descend into the store through a trap door, directly under which stood a hogshead of molasses on one end; so she jumped through the scuttle upon the upper end of the hogshead, when it gave way, and let her into a pool sweeter than any in which she ever before had been immersed."

"There is a bridge at the reservoir just above the mill site, covered with a single stone, twelve feet long, six feet wide, and from twelve to eighteen inches thick, which, it is said, was drawn to its present location one moonlight night, on sleds, over the hills from Purgatory, by twelve yoke of oxen."

"Mr. Sibley was a pioneer, and has left as a monument of his industry nine miles of stonewall which he built or caused to be built.

"One day as Mr. Sibley and his hired man were unloading hay in the barn they heard a screaming in the house and running to see what was the matter found Mrs. Sibley in the cellar. As she stepped off the bottom stair she saw a rattlesnake, which coiled and began to shake its rattles. She was so frightened that she went into convulsions, which continued that day and night, and she declared she would never go in the cellar again, and she never did."

"Unrequited love is said to have been the cause of the derangement of John White, who used to wander around singing verses, 'All for the love of sweet Phebe, my dear!' "

"Master Hall [he was a schoolmaster] used to relate an anecdote to the effect that his father made an exchange with a young minister who had just been settled in one of the neighboring parishes, and who knew nothing about the doctor's family. As he came and was ushered into the parlor, a child was creeping on the floor, so as Mrs. Hall was a very young looking woman, he asked her if that was her first child; she answered, 'Yes, sir, the first of the second dozen.' "

"Dr. Artemus Bullard used to tell how he amputated a sore finger. He put a block on top of a bedpost, ground the chisel very sharp, laid the boy's hand on the block, and with one stroke of the mallet the operation was performed."

"Dr. Hall was a large, fine looking man. His hand was so large that one woman said that it was big enough for Faxon's glove; another, more profane, that it was almost as large as the hand of Providence—Faxon's glove was one hung out in Boston as a glover's sign."

"There used to be great amusement in those general trainings, and their dress parade was a fine sight. Their sham fights were bloodless, and consequently real fun, although they did on one occasion scare all the rats out of the place; they left in the night after the battle. Their tracks were seen a mile distant in a sandy place in the road."

"Edward Anderson enlisted in the late war [Civil War] in the fifteenth Massachusetts volunteers, and was an intrepid soldier. He says he was a coward, because he was afraid to stay at home when his country called, and that he durst not run when under fire."

"Hezekiah never married, but was bedridden sixteen years; he lay in the upper part of the house, and his poor mother attended to his wants by climbing a ladder to his perch all these years. He did not see the sun for fourteen years; at last the roof got leaky, so that the water would run on his bed; then his friends thought it necessary to shingle the house. So, to make him more comfortable they commenced the job. The noise annoyed him very much, so he exclaimed, 'O dear! Stop that noise; it will kill me; I am dying now! If I live half an hour, I shall live as long as God lives.' But they kept driving nails, and 'Kiah' became so mad that he got up and went down the ladder, and soon commenced strolling about the neighborhood. The spell was broken, and so was 'Kiah.' He was good for nothing but to sling invectives. He could not govern his temper, and when excited was gifted in abuse. He once got provoked at Elder Waters, on whom he discharged his battery; when he had fired the last shot in his locker . . . he fell upon his knees and prayed God to give him utterance, saying, 'I have the root of the matter in me, but lack the power of utterance to express my feelings.' "

"David Leland was a man of much public spirit, and gave for a public burying ground the lot now known as the Leland cemetery, in which his remains were buried. But, strange to say, no monument marks his grave. He left a handsome property, and we understand that the heirs, some of them at least, contributed liberally for a monument; but through the neglect of the executor of the will it was never erected. And that unmarked grave remains, an illustration of the frequent forgetfullness of obligation on the part of those who owe the most to the dead."

"In Sutton, Ebenezer Waters, Esq., was a prominent citizen and land surveyor. He gave the bell to the old church. A brother or relative was Elder Waters, a Baptist preacher. As Baptist preachers in these times did not receive salaries, it was necessary that they should procure some secular occupation as the means of support. The elder, as he was called, was an enterprising man of business, a well known and highly respected citizen, and earnest preacher in his denomination. The fact that this good Baptist elder ran a distillery shows how different public sentiment then was as to the manufacturing and use of intoxicating liquors from what it now is. He received the surplus cider of the farmers and converted it into what was called cider brandy, at one time extensively used as a beverage.

"With many other good men, Deacon Bond made cider for the elder's distillery; on one occasion, after having discharged a load of cider, the deacon tarried for the purpose of social chat with the elder. While watching the fire of the distillery, 'Deacon,' said the elder, 'this business furnishes me with some very striking illustrations for my preaching. Here, while attending to the fire, I have time to think and study my discourses. When I want to impress on my hearers the awful subject of future punishment, this big fire which I keep continually burning affords an illustration of the fire of hell which is not quenched. The worm of the distillery reminds me of what Christ has said about the worm that never dies. And then the product, the spirit of the cider, represents the evil spirits by which men are tempted and in danger of being destroyed.' And as the conversation went on, the deacon thought the elder's study, with its fire and worm, and burning fluid, was quite a suggestive place for sermon making. Neither of these good men at that time entertained the slightest suspicion that the business in which they were engaged was not as justifiable as any other occupation."

"There once stood a house directly opposite, owned and occupied by Samuel Putnam. It is said he was one of the five men who drank a barrel of cider in one night, and some locate the feat in this house. Deacon Putnam offered to give him apples, the use of his horse and his cider mill if he would make his own cider. He thanked him and said he could get it cheaper.

"Four men visited him for a social chat. He tapped a fresh barrel of pleasant cider, and they commenced drinking early in the evening and kept at it all night. In the morning, one of them went for another mug, but found the barrel empty. So the five men had the credit of drinking a barrel of cider in one night."

"Mrs. Nathan Palmer came from Salem. When they built the tombs at West Sutton she opposed the enterprise, though her husband was engaged in it. She said they had just such tombs in Salem, and that they were neglected and became dilapidated, and that she had seen dogs carrying dead men's bones taken therefrom through the streets. She said these tombs would fall into ruin in the same way. The tombs were built and for a time were very popular. They even had a 'Day of Resurrection,' on which many already buried were disinterred and placed therein.

"Time passes on, their builders are dead, their friends are gone, the tomb doors fall in, and the bones of the builders are exposed to the dogs as she predicted. The old tombs were complained of as a nuisance, and the court ordered the nuisance abated; so the tombs were torn down and the bones of the dead reinterred."

"Captain Peter Putnam used the old Gould house as a storehouse, granary, etc. Two old men, Daniel Leonard and William Cannon, took lodging in the lower rooms, while the garret was stored with all the usual garret accumulations, such as empty barrels, boxes, etc., besides some two hundred and fifty or three hundred bushels of corn on the ear, which was spread out on the floor to dry.

"In the dead of night when these two old men were fast asleep in the lower rooms of this old two-story house, the door at the head of the stairs, as well as the cellar door in the entry below, both standing open, the garret floor gave way, spilling its entire contents on the single floor directly over their heads, while the crawling corn went rattling down both flights of stairs to the very cellar, giving the poor old sleepers such a scare as is more easily imagined than described.

"Leonard, who was a little, spry old man, caught his pants and went for Captain Putnam, crying, 'Come! come! Captain! The devil to pay at the old house! I guess, but I don't know, I kinder calculate, I don't know, but the devil got Cannon. Come quick, Captain!'

"Captain Putnam aroused, lighted his lantern, and started for the old house. On his way they met Cannon, who, as he was trying to adjust his pants, which, in his trepidation, he had got on wrong side foremost, said, 'I come too, Captain; I thought the devil got Leonard. I couldn't find him nowhere.'

"When the Captain arrived and saw the work he thought it a wonder the Old Fellow had not got them both.

"Cannon was a little deaf. One who was working in the field with him, on a cloudy day, said, 'Mr. Cannon, do you think it is going to rain?' He answered: 'I don't care if I do, a drop.' But it was not eleven and the grog was not there. He hurt one of his thumbs, so that the bone rotted out and made him sick several weeks. For a year or more after it got well he wore a cot on it, and to the salutation of 'Good morning, Mr. Cannon,' would invariably stick up his thumb and say: 'Jes as tender as ye eye.' "

"Mr. Isaac King was a man of great industry and wonderful constitutional strength; he retained his faculties remarkably to the end. Horace Leland said that they were getting in the hay out of the old swamp one day after he was ninety years of age, so he went down to the meadow, took off his shoes, and spread swaths all of the forenoon.

"He fell one day from the great beam in the barn to the barn floor, and being so old they thought his injuries would prove fatal; but the next day he was sitting up in his chair. He said that he fell from the beam and was jarred a little, but thought he should be all right in a day or two, and so he was."

"There once stood in front of this house four large sycamores or buttonwood trees, the most noble of their kind, affording the most grateful shade for man and beast; for in their day, before railways and iron horses came into use, loaded teams and tired droves of panting cattle passed under their extended branches, and were restored and refreshed. Many weary droves from beyond the Connecticut have been halted there to cool their parched tongues. Even the droves from Kentucky have been refreshed by their shade.

"For children and youth, young men and maidens, it was a favorite resort. But what was the fate of these noble trees?

"One who bought the place saw yoke timber in their trunks, so he cut them down and left the spot desolate. The beautiful trees were widely known and much missed and lamented by their numerous admirers."

"The Elliot place was first settled by Joseph Elliot. When he first came to take possession, he was accompanied by two or three young men who came to see the place. After they left, finding himself all alone in the dense wood, he sat down on a large stone and wept like a child. After relieving himself in this way, he aroused his manhood, seized his axe, and commenced felling trees. He soon had a respectable opening; after which he cultivated the land, built him a house, married Jerusha Fuller, and raised an honorable family. The old house, now down, stood near the stone on which he wept."

"Comb making was introduced in town about 1780, by Simeon Carpenter, who came from Attleboro', and was continued by him until 1815. These combs were made of horn, bone, ivory, tin and lead. Deacon Leland remarks, 'Mr. Carpenter says that there was a belief that red hair combed daily with a lead comb would become black; and many people, male and female, have directed him to make them for the purpose of getting rid of carrotty top.' "

Mrs. Josiah Dodd's "mother committed suicide by hanging in the old house. She hung herself with a knot of yarn of her own spinning; it was fastened to a shingle nail so lightly driven that it fell to the floor when she was taken down."

Deacon Reuben Putnam, who was deacon in 1794, named one of his sons Polycarp, and died when the boy was quite small. "When Polycarp was eight years old, he felt that he must do something to help his mother. So he took a bundle of clothes and a cane, and sailed forth to seek his fortune. He first went down the Boston road, stopping at every house to see if they wanted a boy, but no one gave him any encouragement; so he started back and threw his cane up, resolving to go in the direction the cane might point. It directed him, across lots, towards Millbury, so he went in that direction, and at last reached the house of Mr. Jonathan Waters in West Millbury; there he asked Mr. Waters if he wanted a boy. Mr. Waters inquired whose boy he was, and finding him quite intelligent, concluded he would like a boy; so he told him that if his mother approved he might come and work for him. He came and lived with Mr. Waters ten years, and then, by the assistance of friends, went to college, became a Congregational minister and was settled in Great Barrington.

"He married a Miss Brigham of Westboro', and took his mother to his own house and cared for her as long as she lived."

Polycarp, it should be added, changed his name to John Milton Putnam, an act, one would say, that was not entirely without justification.

"Joseph Hall Putnam, Sr., was born in the house opposite, and died here January 6, 1870, aged eighty-nine years, nine months. He was peculiar in his salutations. No matter what the time of day, he said, 'Good morning, sir. Where ye goin'? What ye goin' there for?' He left a large estate."

Ancestral Trees: Yankee Personages

I T IS a Yankee trait to like trees, which are among the things that grow handsomer with age. Dr. Oliver Wendell Holmes, who had an intense and passionate fondness for trees in general and several romantic attachments for certain trees in particular, said that there were old trees scattered about New England worth going a dozen or a score of miles to see. And a journey of that distance in horse-and-buggy days was much more of an undertaking than it is now. Dr. Holmes declared that he had almost worn out a thirty-foot measuring tape on the rough bark of old New England elms and other big trees.

Elms seem to have been his favorites, and these he divided according to size into two classes. Any elm with a girth over twenty feet at five feet above the soil and with a spread of branches a hundred feet across could claim the title of being first class, he said. In his experience most of them did not exceed twenty-two or twenty-three feet in circumference and a hundred and twenty in spread. Elms

of the second class, according to his scale, ranged in girth
from fourteen to eighteen feet, and these he found com-
paratively common.

Among the particular trees which Dr. Holmes mentions
as being noteworthy for size of trunk, spread of limbs,
and muscular development, the great elm at Johnston,
Rhode Island, was in his opinion the first of the first class
of New England elms. It was like a great green cloud
swelling on the horizon, he said, and of Olympian majesty.
But the largest actual girth he had found was in an elm
near the old Bay Path at Springfield, Massachusetts,
though this appeared to have been formed by the merging
of two trunks growing side by side. What the measure-
ments of these trees were he does not state, but it is un-
likely that either exceeded in size the great elm still
standing beside the green in Wethersfield, Connecticut,
which, according to the American Forestry Association, is
the largest American elm in the United States. This noble
tree has a girth of thirty feet, two inches, a limb spread of
one hundred and forty-seven feet, and is ninety-seven feet
tall.

Dr. Holmes knew both the famous Old Elm on Boston
Common and the Washington Elm in Cambridge, but
neither, he said, equaled the Johnston Elm. Before its
fall the Boston Elm was one of the great historical at-
tractions of the city. It was popularly supposed that
witches and malefactors were hanged from its limbs. Tradition also says that Matoonas, one of the sagamores of
King Philip, was shot beneath this tree. After the British
destroyed the famous Liberty Tree at the corner of Essex
and Washington streets, the Old Elm on the Common became a rallying ground for the Sons of Liberty, who
hanged many Tories in effigy from its branches. The tree

measured twenty-four feet in circumference and was seventy-two feet high. Its history was thus summarized on an oval plate on the gate of the iron fence that surrounded the tree.

Washington Elm, Cambridge

The Old Elm

This tree has been standing from an unknown period. It is believed to have existed before the settlement of Boston, being fully grown in 1722. Exhibited marks of age in 1792, and was nearly destroyed by a storm in 1832. Protected by an iron enclosure in 1854.

J. V. C. Smith, Mayor.

Although the limbs of the venerable tree were strengthened with braces and bands, it perished during a storm in February, 1876.

The Washington Elm, which stood on Garden Street, near the northwest corner of the Cambridge Common, was a fair specimen of the tree in the eyes of Dr. Holmes; but in its last years it became a pitiful wreck. It was perhaps even more of an historic shrine than the old Boston Elm. For it was under this majestic vegetable that General Washington is supposed to have taken formal command of the American army on July 3, 1775. His appointment as commander-in-chief was made by the Second Continental Congress in Philadelphia two days before the Battle of Bunker Hill. Philadelphia and Boston were then a week's journey apart. Accompanied by General Philip Schuyler, Washington left Philadelphia on horseback to join the army, and while on the way learned of the Battle of Bunker Hill. When told that the militia had stood up to the British regulars, Washington exclaimed, "The liberties of the country are safe."

As is true of the story of Washington and the cherry tree, there is no direct evidence that when Washington reached Cambridge and took command of the army the ceremony was held near the famous Elm. There was, indeed, no tradition connecting him with the tree until many years after the Revolution. The earliest known picture of the Washington Elm dates only from 1837, but it was soon followed by many others. The subject excited the historical fancy of a horde of artists, who produced a great spate of pictures depicting the ceremony near the elm as they imagined it. It proved especially popular with the illustrators of schoolbooks, who idealized it ludicrously. In an interesting paper read before the Cambridge Historical Society a number of years ago, Samuel F. Batchelder told all the known facts about the Cambridge Elm. Speaking of the outrageous schoolbook illustrations, he said, "Prancing steeds, dipping colors, dear little drummer boys, long rows of troops aligned to a hair's breadth, gorgeously uniformed, and presenting glittering arms with fixed bayonets thrill every youthful heart, while smack in the middle of the front rank stands the Elm, with just room for Washington, flourishing his sword, to ride between it and his immaculate warriors." In one picture, Mr. Batchelder said, Washington appeared to be riding a Shetland pony. Yet these pictures, absurd as many of them were, did as much as anything to promote and establish the legend of the Washington Elm.

It may or may not have been significant that, when President Calvin Coolidge spoke in Cambridge at the one hundred and fiftieth anniversary of Washington's taking command of the army, he did not once mention the tree in his speech. But at the time of this celebration the Washington Elm was no longer standing. Two years before, on October 26, 1923, workingmen engaged in trimming the tree inadvertently pulled the old hulk down.

Crowds of Cambridgians scrambled frantically for relics, but enough of the tree was saved to make many official souvenirs. Pieces of the main trunk were sent to the governors of the forty-eight states, and each state was also presented with a gavel made from the authentic wood. A large section of the tree was sent to Mount Vernon, and many fraternal organizations were given gavels. Altogether about a thousand souvenirs were dispensed.

Very striking must have been the ancient elm on the common or park in Pittsfield, Massachusetts, which was left standing when the original forest was cleared away in the eighteenth century. It was one hundred and twenty-eight feet high, with a clear trunk of ninety feet to the limbs. In shape it resembled nothing so much as a tall sherry glass. Barber, who sketched the tree in 1839, said it never failed to attract the attention of strangers. Dr.

Holmes, who only knew the Pittsfield Elm in its decadence, said it needed a wig of false leaves to make it presentable. The tree was badly scarred by lightning in 1841, and later was further weakened by a second stroke. At last, in 1864, the aged tree had to be removed, and all Pittsfield wept.

Many relics, such as bowls and canes, were made from the wood. But more highly prized now as a souvenir of the tree is the so-called Pittsfield tree plate. In 1825, according to the town historian, a Pittsfield merchant named Allen had a drawing made of the elm and park and sent it to England, where the Staffordshire potters, James and Ralph Clews, used it for a plate design. The print is dark blue, and on the back of the plate is the title, "Winter View of Pittsfield, Massachusetts." It is a typical New England scene, showing the meeting house and other buildings facing on the green with its lofty elm. There is a border of passion flowers and several interesting medallions. China collectors pay a high price for this rare tree plate, still more for the tree platter. In using this arboreal design the Staffordshire potters created a memorial that has done much to keep green the memory of the great Pittsfield Elm.

Trees known in one's youth are remembered always, especially hollow trees, but hardly a person is now alive who could have known in childhood America's most historic tree—the Charter Oak. For the ancient oak was blown down during a summer storm on the night of August 21, 1856. Two Hartford policemen who saw it fall said that when a fierce gust of wind suddenly struck the tree, about one o'clock in the morning, there was a crackling sound from the trunk, and the tree toppled and fell to the ground with a crash that aroused sleepers in the neighborhood.

At the point where it broke off seven feet above the ground it measured twenty-one feet in circumference, and at its base thirty-three feet. So large was its hollow that an entire fire company of twenty-seven full-grown men stood up in it together. How old the tree was when it fell could not be ascertained as its interior had been so eaten away by decay that the rings could not be counted, but it was estimated to be from eight hundred to a thousand years old. It was an outstanding tree when the first settlers arrived in 1635, and there is a legend that the Indians told the English that they had known it for many years and wished that it might be spared when the land was cleared. "It has been the guide of our ancestors for centuries as to the time of planting our corn," they said. "When the leaves are the size of a mouse's ears, then is the time to put the seed in the ground."

The story of this famous tree, in which Captain Wadsworth hid King Charles's charter of the old Colony of Connecticut, is familiar to every schoolboy. It was in the year 1687 that Sir Edmund Andros demanded its surrender in the name of his master, King James the Second. From the first settlement Connecticut had chosen its own rulers and magistrates. It had never had a royal governor or judge, and the rights and privileges it had always enjoyed were confirmed by the charter which Charles Second granted to the colony in 1662. Cotton Mather called it "the freest Charter under the cope of Heaven." But when Charles died in 1685, there was a change in the colonial policy of the home government. James Second appointed Sir Edmund Andros colonial governor of New England, and ordered him to demand the surrender of the Connecticut charter or to seize it. After long consideration the charter or a copy of it was placed on the council table in

Hartford, but, when Sir Edmund reached for the precious document, the lights were suddenly extinguished, and in the ensuing blackout the charter was smuggled away and hidden in the hollow oak. When news of the revolutionary political change in England reached Connecticut, the people of the colony resumed their government under the provisions of the old charter. It had never been vacated by any judgment or decree in the Royal Courts, nor had it been abrogated by any voluntary surrender. On the contrary, the spiriting away and hiding of the charter showed the determination of the people not to surrender it.

At noon on the day the Charter Oak fell, Colt's Armory Band, now the oldest band in the country, played a dirge over the fallen tree, and that evening the bells of Hartford were tolled. Lydia Huntley Sigourney was among the throngs visiting the tree, and the next day wrote a poem on its downfall, in which she mentions the juvenile souvenir hunters looking for acorns to treasure and oak leaves to press between the pages of their Bibles. If the contemporary accounts can be believed, both old and young pillaged the dead tree shamelessly, carrying away much of the sacred wood. Most families living in the vicinity managed to get at least a good chopping block from the Charter Oak.

Yet there was wood enough left for the making of many souvenirs. These included a carved rustic cradle made for Colonel Colt, which was exhibited a few years ago at the Avery Memorial in Hartford with a concealed electrical attachment that automatically rocked the cradle as if it were being moved by a ghostly hand; a gargantuan chair for the presiding officer of the State Senate, still used by the lieutenant governor, and three square pianos, one of which, cut down into a plump-legged table, is in the State

Library. Where the other two pianos are or who is playing boogie-woogie on them today, I do not know. At the Centennial Exhibition at Philadelphia in 1876 many mementoes were displayed, among them a nine-pound ham, said to have been a most mouth-watering imitation, and a game table and set of chessmen. Numerous walking sticks and napkin rings were sold as souvenirs, and bushels of oaken nutmegs—humorous proof, it was declared at the time, that enterprising Yankees did make wooden nutmegs. Even today it is still possible to acquire a relic of the Charter Oak, for a thin, inch-square piece of the wood will be found pasted on page 209 of a book entitled *Souvenir of the Centennial,* published at Hartford in 1877. This book, which is a review of Connecticut's part in the celebration, sells in the secondhand bookshops for a dollar a copy.

Another historic Connecticut tree was the Franklin Oak at South Windsor on the east side of the Connecticut River, a few miles above Hartford. At the time of the Revolution many persons were interned here, among them the royal governor of New Jersey, Sir William Franklin, only son of Benjamin Franklin. He was born about a year after his father's marriage, but the identity of his mother is not known. Benjamin Franklin brought him up in his own home as his son, giving him every advantage. In 1762 William Franklin was made provincial governor of New Jersey, a position which he held at the outbreak of the Revolution. As he chose to remain loyal to the king, he was placed under guard, but the guard was removed when he promised not to leave New Jersey. He kept his promise, but persisted in carrying on his loyalist activities, so in the summer of 1776 he was arrested and taken to

Connecticut, where he remained for more than two years until exchanged in 1778.

He was well treated during his captivity in Connecticut. He was provided with servants and allowed considerable liberty. Two young men of the town, who were assigned to guard him, often accompanied him to his favorite place of resort—a spring of sparkling water near a splendid oak, about one hundred rods from the main road. On this oak, which later bore his name, he made an inscription that remained legible long after he left town. It read:

To the Woodman

Woodman! stay your hand!
Let not the ax's stroke
Deprive this lovely land
Of this monumental oak!
William Franklin.

Many years afterward, in 1830, General George P. Morris embodied this same sentiment in his famous poem, *Woodman, Spare that Tree!* The tree for which the general wrote his plea stood close to what is now the intersection of 98th Street and West End Avenue in New York City.

All over New England are trees or the ghosts of trees to which cling local traditions of the greatest interest. The town of Winterport, Maine, on the Penobscot River, had a Bacon Tree, a giant pine among whose branches the inhabitants hid their provisions of ham and bacon when they heard the British were coming up the river to plunder them. The invaders failed to notice the strange fruit hanging from the limbs of the old pine tree.

A favorite legend which seems incredible is that of the walking stick growing into a tree. Distinguished visitors were always thrusting their canes into the ground outside inns and houses where they had been entertained, leaving the sticks to take root and grow into commemorative trees. Washington and Lafayette are among the magicians who are alleged to have performed this miracle at various places in New England.

An extraordinarily interesting legend concerns the Mike apple, or, as it used to be called, the Rood apple, or Blood apple, which was once very popular in the eastern part of Connecticut, particularly in New London County. This apple was named after Micah Rood, who was an early settler in the town of Franklin, formerly a part of Norwich. On his farm grew the parent Mike apple tree, which bore large, yellow, juicy fruit, but was possessed of a strange peculiarity. In the heart of each apple was a drop of blood. Legend says that this was caused by a murder which was committed beneath the tree. The following local account of the crime and its effect upon the fruit of the tree is from an old history of Franklin.

"Micah Rood, the youngest son of Thomas Rood," it reads, "who was an early settler on the east side of the Shetucket, removed in 1699 to West Farms, and located in Peck Hollow. Micah had upon his farm an apple tree which bore large, fair fruit, but always with a red globule, like a clot of blood, near the center of each apple. The apple, which has become a great favorite in this vicinity, and is called the Mike apple, from its originator, still retains this peculiarity and is the object of much curious inquiry. The drop of blood invariably found in every apple is a standing wonder of childhood's days, and the story of its origin handed down from father to son for over one hundred years, has at length grown to be a fixed tradition, implicitly received.

"As the story runs, a peddler entered the town, vending such costly and luxurious wares as had never before been seen in the settlement. The simple Micah, dazzled by the display, invited the peddler to his house, and at an evil moment plunged a knife to his heart beneath this very tree, so that his life blood flowed down and mingled with the roots. The next spring its blossoms changed from snowy white to red, and in August when the apples came tumbling down, large and yellow and juicy, horror of horrors there hung in every one a drop of blood. There they lay before the terrified Micah, the evidence of his now never to be forgotten deed. With nature in springtime and autumn so strangely prompting the goadings of his conscience, who shall wonder that the simple-hearted Micah should change into a morose and melancholy man, and lead an accursed life? Such was the fact. Time went for naught but the memory of his crime, business was neglected, and soon from a prosperous farmer he became a pauper, dependent on the charities of the community. In 1717 he was glad to increase his slender means by assuming charge of the meeting house, receiving therefor a peck of corn yearly from each family."

The town records tell briefly of Micah's last years and pauper's death.

"July 5, 1727. The inhabitants do now, by their vote, agree to allow to each man that watches with Micah Rood, two shillings per night. Also to those who have attended sd Rood by day three shillings per day.

"December 17, 1728. To Jacob Hyde for digging M. R.'s grave, 0, 4s, od."

These records dispose of the popular version of the legend that Micah Rood hanged himself on the apple tree under which he had murdered the peddler.

The Pilgrim's Progress

IN 1875 Dr. James Hammond Trumbull, president of the Connecticut Historical Society, in anticipation of the one hundredth anniversary of American independence, compiled the following chronological list of major and minor events in American history, particularly New England history, which for interest and information it would be difficult to beat:

1620 Lands on *Plymouth Rock*, and sets up for himself.

1621 Keeps *Thanksgiving*—in no danger of over-eating.

1622 Builds a *Meeting House*.

1623 Proclaims a *Fast Day*.

1628 Cuts down a *May Pole* at Merry Mount, as a rebuke to vain recreations.

1635 Is crowded for accommodations, and stakes out a new farm at *Connecticut*.

1637 Makes war on the *Antinomians*, and the *Pequot Indians*—and whips both.

1638 Starts a *College*, and

1640   Sets up a *Printing Press.*

1643   Goes into a *Confederacy*—the first Colonial Congress.

1648   Lays down the *Cambridge Platform.* Hangs a Witch.

1649   Sets his face against the unchristian custom of wearing long hair, "a thing uncivil and uncomely."

1651   Is rebuked for "intolerable excess and bravery of apparel," and is forbidden to wear gold and silver lace, or other such geegaws.

1652   Coins *Pine Tree Shillings*—and makes the business profitable.

1663   Prints a *Bible* for the Indians.

1680   Buys a "hang-up" *Clock,* and occasionally carries a silver watch that helps him guess the time of day. About this period learns to use *Forks*, at table; a new fashion.

1692   Is scared by *Witches* again, at Salem; but gets the better of them.

1701   Founds *Another College*, which, after a while, settles down at New Haven.

1704   Prints his first *Newspaper*, in Boston.

1705   Tastes *Coffee*, as a luxury, and at his own table.

1708   Constructs another *Platform*,—this time at Saybrook.

1710   Begins to sip *Tea*—very sparingly. It does not come into family use till five and twenty years later.

1711   Puts a letter into his first *Post Office.*

1720   Eats a *Potato*—and takes one home to plant in his garden as a curiosity.

1721   Is *Inoculated* for the Smallpox—not without grave remonstrances from his conservative neighbors. Begins to *Sing by Note,* on Sundays, thereby encountering much opposition and opening a ten years' quarrel.

1740 Manufactures tinned ware, and starts the first *Tin Peddler* on his travels.

1742 Sees *Faneuil Hall* built. The cradle of Liberty is ready to be rocked.

1745 Builds an *Organ;* but does not yet permit it to be played in the Meeting House.

1750 Buys a bushel of *Potatoes* for winter's use—all his friends wondering what he will do with so many.

1755 Puts up a *Franklin Stove* in his best room; and tries one of the newly invented *Lightning Rods.*

1760 About this time begins to wear a collar to his shirt. When he can afford it, takes his wife to meeting in a *Chaise,* instead of on a pillion, as heretofore.

1765 Shows his dislike to *Stamped Paper,* and joins the "Sons of Liberty."

1768 Tries his hand at *Type Founding*—not yet successfully—in Connecticut.

1770 Buys a home-made *Wooden Clock.*

1773 Waters his *Tea,* in Boston Harbor. Plants *Liberty Trees,* wherever he finds good soil.

1774 Lights Boston streets with oil *Lamps*: a novelty (though "New Lights" had been plenty, some years before).

1775 Shows Lord Percy how to march to "Yankee Doodle." Calls at Ticonderoga, to take lodgings for the season. Sends Gen. Putnam (under the command of several colonels) with a small party, to select a site for Bunker Hill monument.

1776 *Brother Jonathan*—as he begins to be called in the family—declares himself Free and Independent.

1780   Buys an *"Umbrillo,"* for Sundays; and whenever he shows it is laughed at for his effeminacy.

1791   Starts a *Cotton Spinning* factory.

1792   Has been raising Silk Worms, in Connecticut; and now gives his minister (not his wife) a homemade silk gown. Buys a *Carpet,* for the *Middle* of the parlor floor.

1793   Invents the *Cotton Gin*—and thereby trebles the value of southern plantations.

1795   Wears *Pantaloons* occasionally, but not when in full dress.

1800   Begins to use *Plates* on the breakfast and tea table.

1802   Has the boys and girls *Vaccinated.*

1806   Tries to burn a piece of *Hard Coal* from Philadelphia; a failure.

1807   Sees a boat go by *Steam,* on the Hudson.

1815   Holds a little *Convention* at Hartford, but doesn't propose to dissolve the Union. Buys one of Terry's patent "Shelf Clocks," for $36.00, and regulates his watch by it.

1817   Sets up a *Stove* in the Meeting House, and builds a fire in it on Sunday; an innovation which is stoutly resisted by many.

1819   Grown bolder, he crosses the Atlantic in a *Steamship.*

1822   Lights *Gas* in Boston (but doesn't light Boston with gas, till 1829). At last, learns how to make Hard Coal burn, and sets a grate in his parlor. Buys a *Steel* Pen (one of Gillott's, sold at $33 per gross.) Has his every-day Shirts made without *Ruffles.*

1825   About this time, puts a *Percussion* Lock on his old musket.

The end of the War of 1812

1826   Buys his wife a pair of queer-shaped *India Rubber* overshoes. Puts on his first *False Collar*. Tries an "Experimental" railroad, by horse power.

1828   Tastes his first *Tomato*—doubtingly. Is told that it is unfashionable to feed himself with his knife— and buys *Silver Forks*, for great occasions.

1833   Rubs his first *Friction Match*—then called a "Lucifer," and afterwards "Loco Foco." Throws away the old Tinder Box, with its flint and steel.

1835   Invents the *Revolver*, and sets about supplying the world with it, as a peacemaker. Tries a *Gold Pen*, but cannot find a good one yet—nor till 1844. Builds a real Railroad, and rides on it.

1837   Gets in a *Panic*—and out again, after free use of "shinplasters."

1838   Adopts the new fashion of putting his letter in *Envelopes* (a fashion which does not fairly prevail till seven years later).

1840   Sits for his *Daguerreotype*, and gets a picture fearfully and wonderfully made. Begins to blow himself up with "Camphene" and "Burning Fluid"; and continues the process for years, with changes of name of the active agent, down to and including "Non-Explosive Kerosene."

1844   Sends his first message by the *Electric Telegraph*.

1847   Buys his wife a *Sewing Machine*—in the vain hope that somehow it will keep the buttons on his shirts. Begins to receive advices from the "Spirit World."

1855   Begins to bore and be bored by the *Hoosac Tunnel*.

1858   Celebrates the laying of the *Ocean Cable;* and sends a friendly message to John Bull. Next week, begins to doubt whether the Cable has been laid, at all.